Contents

Series Introduction:
European Issues in Children's
Identity and Citizenship

A European Education is the final volume in the series European Issues in Children's Identity and Citizenship. The series has arisen from the work of the ERASMUS Thematic Network Project Children's Identity and Citizenship in Europe (CiCe). This network has brought together over 100 University Departments, in 29 European states, all of whom share an interest in the education of professionals who will work with children and young people in the area of social, political and economic education. The Network links many of those who are educating the future teachers, youth workers, social pedagogues and social psychologists in Europe. The CiCe Network began ten years ago, and has been supported by the European Commission's Department of Education and Culture since 1998. It has now completed its third phase of development, and is commencing a fourth phase of activities planned to 2011. We have also formed a CiCe European Association, independent of the Commission, membership of which is open to individuals and institutions. The development of this series has tracked the series of discussions and debates that have been generated by the network we began in the late 1990s, when the European Union had just fifteen members – several of which had only joined the Union five years earlier. It has now reached 2007, with 25 members, three associated states, and negotiations in hand to possibly move the frontiers of the Union to border Iran, Iraq and Syria. But more that this geo-political expansion, the past decade has seen a change in attitudes and constructions of Europe, and this – and its impact on young people – is at the heart of this series.

These volumes have come from our conviction that the changes in contemporary European society are such that we need to examine how the processes of socialisation are adapting to the new contexts. Political, economic and social changes are underway that suggest that we are developing multifaceted and layered identities, that reflect the contingencies of European integration. In particular, children are growing up in this rapidly changing society, and their social behaviour will reflect the dimensions of this new and developing social unit. Identities will probably be rather different: national identities will continue, but alongside new identifications, with sub-national regions and supra-national unions. Our sense of citizenship will also develop in rather different ways than in the past: multiple and nested loyalties will develop, more complex than the simple affiliations of the past. This particular book addresses a wide range of these issues.

The series is designed to discuss and debate the issues concerned with the professional and academic education of teachers, early childhood workers, social pedagogues and the like. They will need to understand the complex issues surrounding the socialisation and social understanding of the young, and to be aware of the similarities and differences in professional practices across Europe. They will need to work with young people learning to be citizens – citizens both of the traditional political entities, and of the developing new polities of Europe.

This final volume differs from its predecessors. It is not an edited collection of papers, but a single-authored book, written by the series editor. It does not, however, necessarily represent the views of either the Network members, nor of the contributors to the earlier volumes; nor is it a resume of what has gone before. It is rather a personal reflection on the road already travelled, and a indication of the topography that may yet be encountered.

CiCe welcomes enquiries from potential members of the Network and the Association. These should be addressed to the CiCe Coordination Unit, at the Institute for Policy Studies in Education, London Metropolitan University, 166-220 Holloway Road, London N7 8DB, United Kingdom.

Alistair Ross
Series Editor

On behalf of the editorial committee: Märta Fulöp, Sören Hegstrup, Riita Korhonen, Beata Krzywosz-Rynkiewicz, Christine Roland-Lévy, Julia Spinthourakis and Ann-Marie Van den dries.

1

A European Education

The title of this book is deliberately ambiguous. In part, it is a discussion of education about Europe, in part it is about how education contributes to the construction of the identities of young people in contemporary Europe, and in part it is about the education that might be thought necessary in order to 'be a European'. It is also framed, inevitably, by the author's own education in, about and for Europe. Finally, it is the concluding volume in a series, and attempts to synthesise some of what has been discussed about how young people learn and are currently learning about their society. It reflects on current changes in society, and particularly European society, as these affect the way in which young people conceptualise and construct their identities and their social relationships with their societies.

This chapter introduces some of the main themes of the book. It is written firmly within the theoretical perspective of social constructivism: it is based on the premise that concepts such as identity, citizenship, nation and Europe are inventions or constructions made by and shared with members of a particular society. As Berger and Luckman argue in their seminal volume in 1966, we socially construct reality through everyday interactions with others. This view is in direct opposition to those who argue that there is something real or essentialist about notions of identity or nation: it will be assumed in this volume that all such ideas only exist in our own consciousness. So I will trace how 'we' (another construct that needs to be untangled) participate in constructing what we conceive of and accept as social reality: the institutions and processes that dynamically

1

create our social world. This is not to advocate cultural relativism: when our construction of knowledge works for us, we pragmatically accept it as a reality that we can (and must) live with. The fact that a truth may only be specific to a particular place and time does not mean that it not a necessary truth for social life to proceed at that place, in that time. Nor am I claiming that, because there are no universal theories, that any one account of reality is as good as any other. Indeed, while Lyotard describes post-modernism as expressing 'an incredulity towards metanarratives' (1984, 24), here I propose a few meta-narratives that the essentialist reader might find incredible.

In the spirit of such social constructivism – and as a pragmatic empiricist – I must here give the reader an account of my construction of my own identity, to allow you the better to interrogate my text.

I could begin with a list of relational identities, sets of practices and descriptions that might define me in your preconceptions of these terms – male, early 60s, husband, father, heterosexual, omnivorous, home-owner, bearded, balding, university professor – or use identity-tags such as middle-class or white. Instead I explore, at a little more length, my locational identities.

I have an English mother, and a Scottish father. This advantages me with an ability to be ambiguous – I generally would describe myself in UK terms as British, though sometimes as Scottish (despite never having lived there). I'd never call myself English (though I have always lived here). London born, brought up in the suburbs, and apart from 4 years studying in Wolverhampton in the late 1960s, always a Londoner. I'm much happier calling myself a Londoner than English. The English bits are solidly English – my mother's ancestors, all 32 of her great-great-great grandparents back to the late 18th Century, were agricultural labouring families from East Anglia. The Scottish bits are as solidly Scottish – all my father's forebears come from the coastal strip of the Highlands, north of Inverness, with the exception of two of his great-grandparents, who came from the isle of Bute, but met, married, and had some of their children in Tasmania in the 1850s.

But I also, and not infrequently, see myself as a European. When I visited Atlanta in the United States I was very conscious that I felt less at home there that I did when in Athens (where I could not read any of the street signs) or in Helsinki (where I could not speak a word of the language). I first visited Europe in the late 1950s, on a camping tour of some West European countries with my family, and recall my mother's bewilderment at the prosperity of France, and her displeasure at the prosperity of Germany (her first husband, a sub-mariner, had been killed in action in 1942). I was a post-war child, conceived within a fortnight of the end of the second world war, and this too has contributed to my identity – the awareness of the comparative prosperity and relative peace of the past 60 years: the only war that I have been caught up in and endangered by was outside Europe. Talking with my contemporaries across Europe, I marvel at the tranquillity of our lives compared to that of our parents – who variously survived Auschwitz, took part in *Maquis* resistance and revenge, bombed Moscow, were evicted penniless from Smyrna to settle in Greece, walked from Armenia to Germany through 1920s Europe, escaped into Warsaw's sewers as the 1944 rising collapsed, acquired Wallenberg visas, were Hitler Youth members, landed in Normandy, and survived. I should mention here the magisterial and, for me, evocative account of Europe's renaissance over my lifetime, Post War, by Tony Judt (2006).

I have also become more European, moving from a rather nationalist perspective in my early teens (I recall being quite anti-European when de Gaulle vetoed English [*sic*] membership of what was then the European Economic Community in 1963, reasoning that if 'they' didn't want 'us', then 'they' constituted a club not worth joining). My views changed when I began hitch-hiking across the length and breadth of Europe late in the 60s, including through East Germany, Yugoslavia and Bulgaria. I remember arriving in Turkey for the first time in 1966, having spent three months following the Mediterranean coast line anti-clockwise – after the Arab countries, Turkey's southernmost towns felt very 'European' and home. More recently, I have visited Europe much more, and particularly been granted privileged insights through working with fellow professionals. I have become acutely aware of the similarities in so much of European culture and practice (and here, Donald Sassoon's *The Culture of the Europeans* (2006) encapsulates both the commonalities and the subtle differences in our popular cultures).

My identity also encompasses, in a way, the differences between the Europeans. In particular, I am conscious of the more liberal way that large parts of Britain approach pluralism and multiculturalism in its make up, and find the way that some continental colleagues refer to second or third generation settlers as migrants distinctly odd. My brief sojourn in Wolverhampton, and the malign influence of the local member of parliament, Enoch Powell (who in 1968 predicted 'rivers of blood' resulting from migration to Britain), helped radicalise my antiracism in this respect. My PhD was on the politics of race in East Africa at the end of the colonial period, and I see reflections of the dated racial arrogance of that period palely reflected in some of the observations of some mainland colleagues.

But I am a European, most definitely. While I acknowledge that much remains to be achieved, I think that the accomplishment of Europe in the field of human rights has been unique – the idea of supranational human rights, enforceable at law, the exportation of rights and the collapse of totalitarianism in Greece, Spain, Portugal and Eastern Europe, the insistence on the abolition of the death penalty, relatively low rates of imprisonment – a vision of Europe perhaps better seen by outsiders than by ourselves (as in Jeremy Rifkin's *The European Dream* (2004)).

This brief self-portrait may help you, the reader, to see how I have constructed my own identity, or more precisely, the identity that I have chosen to share with you, and this in turn may help you to assess how I have constructed the arguments that follow.

This book focuses on contemporary changes in the relationship between the individual, her or his identity and the communities among which the individual lives. It explores the changes in the nature of these communities, and the development of new rights and ideas of rights that are, I argue, at the core of our societies, and about how

4

young people are inducted or educated into these. All of this is set in the particular and unique context of modern Europe. So there is a continuous thread of how identities are fashioned, and how people identify themselves and others, the relations between themselves and others, and society as a whole. I argue that these are social processes, in which young people, interacting socially with others, construct the ways in which they perceive, understand and act and practice with each other. They are not solitary activities. My contention is that we are now witnessing constructions taking place that are qualitatively different from those that have been seen in the past. This in itself is not surprising, but there are nevertheless novel and important aspects. The differences are contingent, both in time and space.

We are living in a society that can be for various reasons be described as post-modern, with new kinds of possibilities, fears, hopes and contiguities. In this increasingly globalised world, we are becoming acclimatised to very different kinds of connectivity, information, knowledge, and contact than have been possible in the past. In particular, we are working in a European context, and this book asserts that there is something special and exceptional about this context. It is neither a sufficient condition for these significantly different forms of learning and understanding, nor is it a necessary condition, but nevertheless it provides a particular contingency that is not at the moment replicated elsewhere in world.

At the core of my argument is a concern with how young people learn to live together in society – which is sometimes called citizenship education. What does it mean to be a citizen, and an *active* citizen? How do we learn to be this? What kinds of pedagogic structures and processes might facilitate this? And what does identity mean in the current context? How do conceptions of citizenship relate to those of identities, and what are the implications for educational policies and practices? Many writers suggest individuals have a multiplicity of identities: does this have consequences for how young people learn about citizenship? This book reviews some of the theoretical bases of identity and citizenship, and their consequences for potential European identity and citizenship, and explores some of the implications for educational policy and practice. It is argued that, in order to be effective, education for active citizenship must address and encompass both the nature of multiple identities and the extension of civic rights to minorities, and in particular that a focus on the possible enhancement of rights will provide a powerful vehicle for learning through deliberative democracy. The current European context provides a particularly useful setting in which active citizenship skills and attitudes can be developed. I move from a discussion of the nature of singular and multiple identities to examine the relationship between identities and citizenship, in both national and European contexts. The connection between citizenship and the development of rights leads to conclusions about educational practices and the development of rights and active citizenship.

'Political education' is not a term in frequent use today: for many years it has been regarded with suspicion. In much of Eastern Europe it is now associated with the educational policies of the former regimes and as akin to indoctrination. In western Europe and North America, it has been criticised variously as impossible, unnecessary and an interference with the liberties of the individual and/or family (see, for example, Davies, 1994, 1999). Political learning is perceived of as *being* controversial, and as *being about* the controversial. I examine both charges, and argue that young people, throughout their education, need to be introduced to the controversial. There has been a rather fitful development of political education in recent decades, and I try to develop a practical model of how teachers can use controversial issues to develop political understanding.

Both educational and political arguments are sometimes advanced against political education for pupils. From an educational perspective, it has been argued that children are incapable of the sort of complex social thinking that is necessary to understand politics. From the political viewpoint, it is asserted that it is impossible to tackle politics in an unbiased, even-handed way, and should therefore not be attempted, and that any political understanding should not be formally transmitted by the educational system, but should properly be absorbed from family, the media and the political institutions themselves. Both of these sets of arguments are flawed, and there has been substantial resurgence of interest in this area, often through forms of 'rebranding' – as civics education, citizenship education, or political literacy.

I begin the next chapter with a discussion about the relationship between identity, citizenship and education. Broadly speaking, many inhabitants of Europe are now beginning to express themselves – perhaps partially, perhaps hesitantly, perhaps only occasionally – as European. What does this imply about their education, and what does it suggest about the future of education? Often seen as a process for reproducing social values and imbalances, education can sometimes transform and change The curriculum is frequently generated from past practices and embeds invented traditions, but it *can* sometimes challenge these, or even bypass them. Identities are not fixed essentials, but malleable, and in chapter three I analyse various ways in which the identity and concept of Europe has changed. In particular, I try to identify moments at which there has been a significant shift in the semantics of the boundaries of identity, as Europe in the past moved from xenophobia to colonialism and empire: I also suggest that there has been a recent rejection of the past, and that we are now witnessing a different dimension in the nature of the 'othering' that is associated with identity boundaries. Rather than the other being defined territorially, as in the past, Europe in now defining the other temporally – 'the other' for Europe is now the past.

To participate in a community, be it defined territorially (as in a nation state) or defined temporally (as I suggest Europe now is) requires some sense of belonging: identification with the community requires, rather than implies, participation. But this participation can have various degrees or levels of activity or inactivity. Chapter four explores active and passive citizenship, and suggests that the cosmopolitan nature of modern society, and particularly of modern European society, requires activism on the part of its members. In chapter five I analyse the necessary elements of an active citizenship education: the processes, the values and the skills that are necessary. In particular, I argue that young people are most likely to be fired up and enthused by considering issues of fairness, justice and equity, and that an issues-based curriculum is best placed to provide such a forum.

The European Union can be argued as predicated upon a creative tension between cooperation and competition. The educational processes set out so far in my argument have been premised on cooperative learning, within a certain competitive frame. Chapter six therefore explores these two dynamics, competition and cooperation, in a variety of social settings, and suggests that they should be seen as complementary, rather than antithetical.

At this point, my argument returns to the issue of identities. I suggest that identity in the contemporary or post-modern context is rather more complex than it was in the past, and that most people are now expressing multiple identities, where the reference points and boundaries to their identities are, to an extent, malleable and contingent upon the particular social setting in which they find themselves. Identities may overlap, may be nested, may be discrete. Identities are not merely constructed – non-essentialised, created in the social market – but are also hyphenated, hybridised, shifting from moment to moment, from place to place, from social setting to social setting. This does not make us schizophrenics, but allows the flexibility to be – for example, British, or Scottish, or European (and also to be not English).

If this argument is accepted, then the question that follows is: how do we develop such different identities? Chapter eight teases out the relationship between identity, experience and learning. The idea of situated learning, as a form of apprenticeship or induction into a community, is used to propose a framework within which young people might negotiate their identities and belonging to communities.

Before taking this to a more practical level, in chapter nine I introduce the development of human rights and their relationship to citizenship. These rights, I argue, are not static, but have moved through a series of stages over several centuries, and are still moving on. There are rights yet to be won, over injustices that are as yet only partially articulated, or are still inchoate. The particular significance of this, I argue, is that this area is particularly suitable for active learning and thus for learning to be an active citizen. If we confine learning about rights to a recitation of facts about rights fought for and won long ago, we are risking turning young people's understanding of rights into a litany of past battles. Worse, it can suggest a teleological journey that has been completed: we have come the distance, and achieved in the glorious present all that needs to be achieved. Focusing on injustices yet to be resolved achieves many goals: it latches on to young people's sense of justice; it acknowledges current imperfections; and above all, it provides a real location for active learning, helping young people understand how they can work to improve and define rights. This is active learning for active citizenship.

The concluding chapters consider how this can be practically achieved. What are the core principles of curriculum design in this area? Reviewing critical studies of the practice of citizenship curriculum design, various key elements are identified that inform approaches to progression and differentiation. These include deliberative debate, based on an approach to values that is set in the ethos of the whole school: a radical reordering of traditional teacher-learner relationship, based on respect for the learner and the empowering of experiences. Two critical strategies emerge: the imperative of a whole school approach towards determining values, structures, planning and attitudes towards pupils' identities and rights; and the need for a radical classroom dialogic, based on a relationship of respect for the learner.

Finally, the argument returns to European citizenship. What does it mean to have a European identity? How does this match with other, alternative identities, which may be nested within Europe or not? What curricular policies will illuminate these issues, what pedagogic processes will help learning, and what educational structures will provide the necessary context? To return to the initial debate: are Europeans expressing a European identity? What does this say about their citizenship, and how are younger people different in the way that they express it?

2

Education for Citizenship in the European context: reproduction and change

The Europe Union is now a well-established entity, a real political institution rather than simply an aspiration. It is something to which many people have a sense that they belong. When asked in 2004 whether they saw themselves as having a European or partially European identity, a representative sample in various European countries responded as shown in Table 2.1.

With the exception of the UK, a majority of each of these populations saw their identities as containing at least a partial European dimension, and a tenth of them put European first. This tendency is stronger among younger people in all countries (Lutz *et al*, 2006). Such a finding would have been inconceivable sixty years ago. It is

Table 2.1: Response to the question 'In the near future do you see yourself as...?'

(answers expressed as a percentage of each national sample)

	All EU	DK	FR	DE	IT	LX	ES	UK
Wholly as a member of my national state	41	43	29	38	28	27	32	62
A member of my national state and a European	46	51	54	46	56	39	58	27
A European and a member of my national state	6	4	8	8	8	12	4	4
Wholly as a European	4	1	6	6	3	18	3	4

Source: Eurobarometer EB61, April 2004 (European Union Research Group, 2004)

11

not simply a consequence of the formation of the European Union: people in countries not in the Union express similar aspirations, and clearly even 40 years of membership of the Union leaves a substantial proportion of the UK population cold. Europeanness is something that at least partially transcends and is independent of the Union, and is something to which younger people in particular appear more attuned. How and why do some young people develop this sense of identity?

One of the central themes of this series has been the connection between identity and citizenship. What we know of citizenship education, and particularly of citizenship education in Europe, may help explain how this curriculum area might contribute to the ways in which young people express their sense of identity. There are various expositions on the purpose of education, and the role and form of education for citizenship may be very different depending in how a particular society defines as the rationale for schooling and education.

The individuals surveyed in Table 2.1 had different conceptions of their identities as Europeans. But the great majority of them *were* European citizens. Citizenship of the Union was introduced in the 1993 Maastricht Treaty (European Union, 1993) and reaffirmed in the Treaty of Nice (European Union, 2000a). Every person who is a national of a member state of the Union is also a European Union citizen. Articles 17 and 21 of the 1992 treaty give citizens four main rights, including protections – passive rights – and political control – active rights:

1. The right to move freely among, and stay in, other member states.

2. The right to vote and stand for election in local and European Parliament elections in the member state where one lives. Members of the European Parliament are directly elected by citizens of the various member states, and the Parliament is a cross-state representative body, whose power over European Union legislation has gradually increased.

European citizenship gives new political rights to those who have used opportunities for mobility.

3. Protection in non-EU countries by the diplomatic staff other member states, if one's own member state is not represented.

4. The right to petition the European Parliament, and to petition the European Ombudsman.

European Union citizenship does not replace national citizenship, but complements it. Citizens of Member States are not regarded as foreigners when they travel and live in European Union countries other than their own (Preuss, 1996, p139).

W J M Mackenzie (1978) argues that citizenship is fundamentally linked to a sense of place, and must therefore include references to the particular community or communities of which one might be considered a citizen. What does, and what should, the citizenship curriculum in European countries attempt to do?

Heaton and Oliver (1994) set some challenging goals for the outcomes of citizenship education. Pupils should be able to

■ actively practise 'civic virtue and good citizenship'

■ enjoy – but not exploit – civil and political rights

■ contribute to and receive social and economic benefits

■ not discriminate against others

■ experiences non-exclusive multiple citizenship

■ teach citizenship to others (derived from Heater and Oliver, 1994, p6)

Another indication of what might be considered as the purposes of both education and of the citizenship curriculum, and as to how these should be organised and ordered into a coherent and logical structure, can be found in a pioneer writer on citizenship, Aristotle, on the purposes of education:

In modern times there are opposing views about the tasks to be set, for there are no generally accepted assumptions about what the

13

young should learn, either for their own virtue or for the best life; nor is it yet clear whether their education ought to be conducted with more concern for the intellect than for the character or soul ... It is by no means certain whether training should be directed at things useful in life, or at those most conducive to virtue, or at exceptional accomplishments. Aristotle, 1966 *The Politics*, Book VIII, Chapter ii, 1337a33

A basic assumption might be that citizenship education should be for all pupils, and that it is intended to make all of them aware of citizenship as 'a thing useful for life', and its practice 'conducive to virtue'. It follows that we are not concerned – as might be the case in many other aspects of the curriculum – in grading or ranking pupils as more or less successful citizens. The exigencies of contemporary society mean that we cannot afford a single 'failed citizen', and that all must succeed. 'Exceptional accomplishments' in citizenship will be necessary for some, but not all, members of society, but education toward such contributions lies beyond the consideration of core citizenship education for all.

This does not, however, mean that the curriculum need not progress pupils through different levels of skill and understanding, that will hone and refine sensibilities and feelings through sequences of learning activities, nor that we need not assess and evaluate progression. Responsible teaching requires all of these aspects to be considered, but with the goal of ensuring that *all* acquire the competences of citizenship, rather than of distinguishing between democratic sheep and uncivic goats. 'Democratic sheep' may be tautologous; but noncitizens, or even poorly-skilled citizens, are potentially a danger to the rest.

As the quotation from Aristotle suggests, there has been a longstanding debate about the purposes and nature of education. Education has generally been perceived as a powerful social tool, but sometimes as a tool that can be used to conserve, preserve and transmit an established culture and social structure, and at other times as a mechanism that can transform and change a culture, and be an agent for social mobility. Aristotle identified three variations that remain valid in most analyses of contemporary educational systems, curricula and purposes. Each has particular implications for what kind of citizenship education should be offered.

Firstly, he identified a utilitarian or instrumental argument for education: training directed at the useful things in life. An instrumental education may be one designed to produce citizens that are 'useful' to a society – with the necessary knowledge and skills to fill particular occupational niches in an economy, for example, or with suitable attitudes of deference to and acceptance of authority. This implies that a national government, or other authority supplying or regulating educational provision, would have utilitarian concerns in promoting citizenship education. This might mean (in a relatively benign context) trying to persuade pupils that they should vote in election, thus addressing the 'democratic deficit'; or, in less benign contexts, creating subservient attitudes that accept the views and policies of the authorities. The question that needs to be asked in this context is 'useful to whom?' The benefits to the individual of being a critically informed and active citizen may be rather different from the benefits to an authoritarian regime of having docile citizens that accept their decisions – and the kinds of citizenship education that are devised in these two contexts will be divergent. Or an instrumental education may be one that addresses the student's view of what will be useful, or their parents' views of this.

Secondly, Aristotle suggested that education may be directed to support 'virtue' (*eudaimonia*: this is also variously translated as 'happiness' or 'flourishing' and occasionally as 'well-being'). The Stanford Encyclopedia of Philosophy (Zalta, 2007) points out that while animals and even plants can flourish, *eudaimonia* is possibly only for rational beings; and that 'happiness' implies something subjective. Virtue is a multi-faceted disposition to behave in a particularly pro-social manner: an educational system that encouraged this would focus on the development of the individual and the processes by which their individuality was formed in relation to others in society. Citizenship education in such a context might be directed at helping pupils understand, appreciate and promote a human rights agenda, both in respect of their own rights and in safeguarding and extending the rights of others. The European Union context here offers a very distinctive and particular agenda for rights education, as the only supranational authority with the jurisdiction to legally enforce various human rights: various aspects of this will be explored in more detail in chapters six and nine.

Aristotle's third possible justification for education was the development of 'exceptional accomplishments' (which requires both the notion of an agreed definition of what 'an accomplishment' is – in other words, a determination of cultural knowledge – and some form of comparison or competition that would define the exceptional). Education in such a context would be concerned with the transmission of the content of culture, and in a citizenship context, civic culture. While Almond and Verba, the classic analysts of the civic culture (1963), questioned the processes of socialisation into the civic culture, asserting that civic culture is transmitted by a complex mix of social institutions – family, peers, school, work, and the political system itself – rather than through school, it can equally be argued that schools could have specific roles in introducing a range of political cultures – local, regional, national and supra-national – to pupils.

These three forms are, of course, essentialised types rather than descriptions of actual practice. Most educational systems combine elements of all three rationales, though possibly in varying proportions. Any modern educational system (and indeed, most in history) would claim to be transmitting cultural knowledge, to be developing the individual and to be meeting the social objective of preparing a skilled and industrious workforce. The emphasis given to any of these three objectives might vary, but all will be present in some form or other. Each of the three dimensions is concerned with the possible relationship between the educational system and the wider societies or cultures within which it is located – which could be a local culture, a national society, or a European society. Broadly, there are two models of this relationship.

Emile Durkheim characterised education as 'the image and reflection of society. It imitates and reproduces the latter in an abbreviated form; it does not create it' (1897, p372). He argued that education was 'the means by which society prepares, within the children, the essential conditions for its very existence.' This view holds that education essentially reflects and reproduces the society in which it is embedded: 'Society draws for us the portrait of the kind of man [sic] we should be, and in this portrait all the peculiarities of its organisation come to be reflected' (1956, p65). This functionalist view is still common: 'all societies have the task of passing on to the next generation the knowledge and skills regarded as particularly worthwhile; ... societies achieve this by means of ... education' (Lawton and Gordon, 1996, p10). This view emphasises stability, and views society as essentially homogeneous and static. The reflection is mirror-like and results in self-replication. We learn who we are to be: we are what we have learned to be. Nations thus reproduce, or expect to reproduce, national characteristics through the schooling process. How nations might change, or how new organisations (such as a new country, like Montenegro, or a new union, such as Europe) might become established is problematic in such a narration.

John Dewey proposed an alternative and transformative model of education. The school process should not only promote social equality, so that 'each individual gets an opportunity to escape from the limitations of the social group in which he was born, and come into contact with a broader environment (1907, p20), but also develops and extends the individual – 'it creates a desire for continued growth and supplies the means for making the desire effective in fact' (p50). These egalitarian and developmental functions partly derived from Dewey's view of knowledge as something that had be constructed by the learner as an active experimenter. More recently, John Rawls has also argued that education has such an egalitarian and developmental function:

> resources for education are not to be allocated solely or necessarily
> mainly according to their return as estimated in producing trained

abilities, but also according to their worth in enriching the personal and social life of citizens, including here the less favoured (Rawls, 1971, p107)

We decide whom we would like to learn to be: we are what we choose to learn. This model allows considerable latitude and flexibility to the learner in the context of citizenship and socio-political identity. States that felt their hegemonic hold over their citizens was in dispute or weakened might resist such an educational approach, whereas new political entities might be particularly anxious to introduce young people to new ways of experimenting with their identity.

Thus the social behaviour that is determined within the discourse of the classroom has potential to be either the simple reproduction of existing patterns of behaviour or to be transformative: and there has been considerable debate about schooling and social and cultural reproduction.

Many observers suggest that education does not act – or has not acted – to transform society. Jencks (1972) argued that education has not been an equalising influence, and that not only have the better-off appropriated far more than their share of publicly funded educational resources for their children, but that even if all pupils had the same educational resources, there would be no substantial change towards equalities of income as a consequence. Raymond Williams argued that 'the common prescription of education, as the key to change, ignores the fact that the form and content of education are affected, and in some cases determined, by the actual systems of decision and maintenance' (Williams, 1961, p120). Political (decision) and economic (maintenance) structures tend to prescribe the composition of the curriculum and the systems by which it is delivered, in ways that minimise the possibility of societal or economic change. Michael Apple develops this further, concluding that schools contribute to inequality because they are *intentionally* organised to unequally distribute particular kinds of knowledge (1990, p43). Other studies suggested that individual schools might make a difference to educational attainment. In a longitudinal study of English secondary schools by Rutter and others it was suggested that there were aspects

18

of a school's activities that *did* influence academic attainment: the atmosphere of cooperation, the organisation of coursework and the quality of pupil-teacher relationships were important variables that were within the control of the school. Adjusting for social class factors, Rutter suggested that some schools achieved significantly better than others, and that a superior learning environment could not simply be equated with schools that were materially better resourced (Rutter *et al.*, 1979).

Apple argues that this reproduction is not a conspiracy to deprive, but a 'logical necessity' to maintain the unequal social order (1990, p40). A schooling system which credentialises a particular proportion of the population roughly equivalent to the needs of the division of labour (and therefore de-credentialises the rest) is an almost natural way of maintaining the economic and cultural imbalance on which these societies are built. Apple goes on to suggest that because education legitimises the economic and social order, it is an *active* force, and not merely engaged in passively mirroring society (1990, p42). The content of education, the ethos in which it is presented, and the structures through which it is delivered are all part of the intimacy education has with the socio-economic order of society. Education delivers the economic hierarchies necessary for each generation, using structures to produce and reproduce different forms of official knowledge in different social orders, and to inculcate pupils to accept the uneven power structure that lies behind this as being normal and common sense.

One of the best known expositions of the nature and workings of the hidden curriculum in the context of the political economy was made by Bowles and Gintis (1976, 1988). To them, education is simply a response to the capitalist system, transmitting technical and social skills (through the overt curriculum), and inculcating discipline and respect for authority (through the hidden curriculum). The social relations of the means of production correspond to the social relations of schooling, and this, they argue, is no coincidence.

> The school is a bureaucratic order, with hierarchical authority, rule
> orientation, stratification by 'ability' as well as by age, role

> differentiation by sex (physical education, home economics, etc.), and a system of external incentives (marks, promises of promotion, and threat of failure) much like pay and status in the sphere of work. (Bowles and Gintis, 1976, p87)

It is not just that schools reproduce the personality types required by capitalist production – 'those at the base of the hierarchy requiring a heavy emphasis on obedience and rules, and those at the top, where the discretionary scope is considerable, requiring a greater ability to make decisions on the basis of well-internalised norms' (p87) – this is the very *purpose* of the school. Alienation and anomie are *necessary* outcomes of this schooling, not merely incidental to the incompatibility of the cultures of the primary and secondary socialisers (Gramsci, 1971; Berger and Luckman, 1966). This rather gloomy view might suggest that schools in capitalist societies might find it hard to promote civic virtues and prosocial behaviour. In some of their more recent writing, Gintis, Bowles *et al* (2003) suggest that people exhibit strong reciprocity, or a willingness to reward good behaviour even when doing this brings them no material benefit. Despite their schooling, individuals often go beyond self-interest and act in the common good, through a sense of equity: this will be explored at greater length in chapter six.

Pierre Bourdieu's theory of cultural capital includes both cultural production and reproduction in schools. The cultural capital of the middle class is expressed through its habits of thought, assumptions and complexions, that are particularly cultivated and expressed by the school system: the school inculcates, partly through the formal but particularly through the informal curriculum, 'not so much with particular arid particularised schemes of thought as with that general disposition which engenders particular schemes, which may then be applied in different domains of thought and action' (Bourdieu, 1971, p184). This cultural capital is used as a mechanism to filter pupils to particular positions within the hierarchy of capitalist society. Schools re-create the social and economic hierarchies of the society in which they are embedded, not only through the processes of selection and teaching but also by judging and comparing these activities against the cultural capital held by the middle class. In so doing, they effectively discriminate against all those children who have not had access to such capital. 'By taking all children as equal, while implicitly favouring those who have already acquired the linguistic and cultural competencies to handle a middle class culture, schools take as natural what is essentially social gift, ie cultural capital' (Dale *et al*: 1976, p4). As Bourdieu puts it, 'the cultural capital and the ethos, as they take shape, combine to determine behaviour and attitude to school which make up the differential principle of elimination operating for children of different social classes' (Bourdieu, 1974, p36). Applying the same cultural criteria in an equal way favours the students who have been previously socialised into the particularly favoured culture.

This is a wide-ranging claim. It implies that the 'nature versus nurture' debate is irrelevant, because we largely do not choose our identity – or indeed, *cannot* choose our identity.

> We receive the cultural identity which has been handed down to us from previous generations. ...as we grow older, we modify the identity we have inherited. The identity is not intrinsic but the scope for changing it is circumscribed by the social expectations of the group with which we are associated. By our actions we informally reinforce our inherited group affiliation. (Robbins, 1990, p174)

In this model, we are formally socialised by the system of education. The state establishes a schooling system to give the particular training or instruction necessary for the changing labour market. The schooling system may also seek to build in the whole population of the state an identity or association with the nation-state, that is in some way parallel to, or equivalent to, the group or class affiliations. States are themselves artificial or invented constructs (see eg Colley, 1992; Hobsbawm and Ranger, 1983) that seek to construct uniform social identities within their synthetic boundaries. Ernest Renan's celebrated Sorbonne lecture of 1882, asked 'What is a nation?' He argued that a nation could not be defined in terms of race, language, religion, interest group or a naturally defined territory – indeed, in terms of any substantive attributes (Renan, 1882). Ulrich Beck and Edgar Grande conclude that the same lack of significant characteristics is true of the concept of Europe (2007, p7).

These various models of education broadly translate into different policies concerning the curriculum. Dividing the curriculum in this way can, as has been shown, be traced back to Aristotle: in more recent curriculum analysis, a variety of names and labels have been used. The content-based curriculum (Ross, 2000) has also been described as subject-based and knowledge-based (Lawton, 1975), as the academic curriculum (Goodson, 1987), and in primary education as a preparatory curriculum designed to lead to the traditional subject curriculum (Blyth 1967). The objectives-driven curriculum was designated society-centred (Lawton), utilitarian (Goodson), elementary (Blyth) and technocratic (Golby, 1989). The final variety has been variously called child-centred (Lawton), pedagogic (Goodson), developmental (Blyth) and child-centred progressivism (Golby). Ross (2000) has extensively analysed each of these curriculum models, respectively using the terms content-driven, objectives-driven and process-driven.

Citizenship is the relationship between the individual and society, between the self and others. The complexity we now face is that individuals can simultaneously belong to a number of different societies which may intersect, be nested, or be independent of each other. I can thus legitimately describe myself as a Londoner, British, Scottish, and a European: these are either nested or intersect (Scottishness is the one that intersects; all in some ways are nested). Each of these societies requires a different relationship between myself and the social group, and my citizenship education requires sufficient flexibility so that I can behave in a civic manner in each of these contexts.

The curriculum as a whole, and the citizenship curriculum in particular, must reflect this: helping the individual understand both her own identity and the nature of the societies she inhabits, and, most importantly, how she can manage the complex relationship of rights and responsibilities that exist between the two in each of her societies. Audigier underlines the magnitude and scope of this: 'Since the citizen is an informed and responsible person, capable of taking part in public debate and making choices, nothing of what is

22

human should be unfamiliar to him [*sic*], nothing of what is experienced in society should be foreign to democratic citizenship' (1998, p13). This opens the way for a vast range of exhilarating and stimulating work, drawing from the whole canvass of contemporary political and social debate. In one sense, the content of the citizenship curriculum is straightforward, based on all the social and political debates of the day. In the slogan of a UK populist newspaper, 'all human life is there'. What is critical however, and the major thrust of this book, are the conditions and means by which these issues are debated, argued, analysed and acted upon by pupils. How do we order this into some kind of coherence? How do we ensure that pupils broaden and enhance their civic skills, their values and their moral susceptibilities in both a national and a European context? Table 2.1 above shows that in many countries in Europe a majority of the population, and particularly of younger people, are able to see themselves as belonging to, and probably operating in, a variety of political-social contexts.

While many politicians would settle for a passive citizen, who votes, subscribes to the state, and obeys the law, many others – including perhaps most teachers – would hope to empower active citizens, who critically engage with and seek to affect the course of social events. This critical distinction between active citizenship and passive citizenship will be analysed later (in chapter four), particularly in terms of its implications for curriculum planning. This necessitates some discussion of the key elements within a citizenship curriculum, and in particular the use of categories such as values and attitudes, skills and competences, knowledge and understanding and creativity and enterprise to analyse this. The significance of these categories varies in how they affect planning progression, attainment and differentiation, particularly in terms of encouraging active, as opposed to passive, citizenship. Two significant core concerns of citizenship education are those of identities and of rights, and each of these can be related to key values, skills and knowledge in active citizenship education.

Before exploring these issues, however, it will be helpful to characterise what is meant by European identity. There are no unique substantive attributes to Europe – it is impossible to define precisely in terms of geographical area (compare, for example, the nations participating in the European Song Contest and those in the European Football Cup), of or of peoples, or of language. In some traditions, groups have defined themselves in terms of 'the other'. Edward Said suggests the West has often defined itself against the exotic and oriental:

> [Orientalism] is fundamentally a political doctrine willed over the Orient because the Orient was weaker than the West, which elided the Orient's difference with its weakness . . . .. As a cultural apparatus Orientalism is all aggression, activity, judgment, will-to-truth, and knowledge. (Said, 1978, p204)

Said argued about what he called Orientalism that it was 'not [that it is] a misrepresentation of some Oriental essence – in which I do not for a moment believe – but that it operates as representations usually do, for a purpose, according to a tendency, in a specific historical, intellectual, and even economic setting' (1978, p273). Linda Colley argues persuasively that the United Kingdom in the eighteenth century defined itself against the French as 'the other' (Colley, 1992), cleverly and ambiguously describing the process as 'forging'. But there are other ways of defining a group identity, and the following chapter argues that the European identity had some particular, albeit unsubstantive, characteristics that give it peculiar and important qualities – qualities that are particularly important in discussions on citizenship and identity. Citizenship and identity can be – are – qualitatively different in the context of the European Union. In some senses, the next chapter may appear to be a historical digression, but it offers a conceptualisation of why a European identity is unusual, uncommon and extraordinary.

3
Forging European Identities

One form of identity is expressed in the way in which individuals label themselves as members of a particular group – for example, of a country, or with a particular ethnicity, or in terms of gender, class, culture or religion. This makes it possible to discuss a national identity, or a class identity, or so on, and the identity of such groups is constructed around the characteristics that each member thinks they have in common with all the others who identify themselves with the same group. National characteristics are the common attributes of the people who profess to be members of that nation: they are thus social constructs, that are contingent on the particular circumstances of time, place and population. Most people in contemporary societies are members of many groups, and an individual may have a number of identities that intersect, so can select which identity they profess in different contexts. These identities are a function of historical and cultural circumstances: although a social construction created by circumstances, it nonetheless has real consequences for people's behaviour (Berger and Luckmann, 1966).

Identities in a relatively simple society that has little interaction with other groups might be traditionally prescribed within a limited range of possibilities, perhaps defined by gender, social status and familial relationship. Without significant contact or awareness of other groups, there would be little point in defining one's identity in relation to those other groups. Thus many peasant or subsistence-based societies in the past would have defined their identities without reference to nationality, for example. The changes brought about by modernity (say from the early sixteenth century in many parts of Europe) – such as the developments in technology, exploration, communications, travel, science, education and the arts – created far more complex societies, in which a much greater range of identities became possible. Identity moved from being ascribed (by birth, location, etc) to include achieved characteristics, and possibilities of choice of more numerous identities. Shotter and Gergen have argued that changes in kinds of identity develop in parallel to cultural changes: modernity brought a set of identities defined around rationalism, and postmodernity brought identities that developed around the relational self (Shotter and Gergen, 1990; Giddens, 1991). Some of the aspects of how individuals learn to construct their various singular and multiple identities are considered in greater detail in a later chapter.

This chapter explores how one kind of identity – the European – has been constructed in different periods, and in particular examines some of the critical moments that triggered different aspects of the construction. This exploration will help illuminate the various ways in which identities can be constructed, and the potential consequences of different ways of demonstrating or manifesting these identities, and the changing conceptualisation of what it means to be European. In particular, I hope to clarify the most recent reconstruction of European identities, currently still in progress, showing how each of the previous moments of constructions have had consequences for the present. This is not intended to imply a direct or casual relationship between each of these events and the construction of forms of European identities, but rather to show that each in some way contributed to significant changes in how many people in Europe identified themselves. It is not suggested that these changes were in any way inevitable or linked to some great teleological narrative about the emergence of 'the European identity'. These critical moments each prefaced significant reconstructions in the way Europeans thought about themselves, and have contributed to the situation in which we now find ourselves: they tell us something about who some of us think we are now.

The first critical event occurred in about 490-480 BCE, around the events known as the Persian Wars. Before this time, the Greeks do not appear to have envisaged their neighbours as enemies. Homer treated Greeks and Trojans as equals in the Illiad. The term barbarian, or non-Greek, simply meant foreigner, specifically some-one who does not speak Greek: Homer uses it with no negative connotations. The attitude to others – and particular easterners -and the use of the word barbarian shifted dramatically in about 480 BCE.

Cyrus the Great had established a Persian state sixty years earlier, in the process occupying most of Asia Minor His successor, Darius, annexed the Aegean islands. The Persians were conciliatory: tribute was replaced with a progressive tax based on the wealth of each city, democracies were established in some of the Ionian city-states, prisoners were returned, and Darius encouraged the local Persian nobility to participate in Greek religious practices. Persian and Greek nobility began to intermarry, and Persian nobles' children were given Greek names. Darius' policies were publicised in main-land Greece, so that when Darius demanded Greek submission in 491, most city-states initially accepted the offer, Athens and Sparta being the significant exceptions.

The Persians sent a large army that landed near Marathon. The Athenians and their sole allies, the Plataeans, thoroughly defeated the invading forces: the effects were significant for both sides. By successfully defying the superior Persian forces they showed the other Greek cities that resistance was possible, and several city-states renounced their submission to Persia and joined the Athenians and Spartans. The impact on the Persians of the first defeat of Persian infantry forces since before Cyrus was to signal their in-adequacy at sea and to threaten their holdings in the western part of their empire. Darius set about raising an invasion force, which was taken on by his son Xerxes on his death. It is estimated this may have been between 200,000 and 250,000 strong (Herodotus says 2.5 million). The army marched to the Hellespont, where 674 triremes were lashed together to form two bridges, over which the cavalry and foot soldiers crossed. It took four months for the army and fleet to move towards Attica. The Greek and Spartan forces divided to cover the possible approaches, and just 300 Spartans were assembled when the Persian army arrived at the pass of Thermopylae. The Spartans were eventually overcome, but the battle allowed the Greek forces to regroup, and defeat the weakened Persian forces at Platae. The fleets met at Salamis: the Persian triremes were routed, and the Persians withdrew from Attica for good.

The Persian civilisation was at that time elaborate and advanced in comparison to the Greek. Darius' government codified data about the empire, and devised a universal legal system. The practice of slavery was generally banned, and they freed the Jews held at Babylon. The new capital, Persepolis, was built by paid workers rather than slaves. The 2,500-kilometer Royal Road from Susa to Sardis allowed relays of mounted couriers to reach the remotest areas within fifteen days. Darius also initiated a central economy based on a silver and gold coinage system, leading to extensive trading and the exchange of commodities: trade tariffs were one of the empire's main sources of revenue. The mathematical system they had developed from the Babylonians was more advanced than that of anywhere else at the time.

One of their most significant contributions may be the Cyrus Cylinder, described as the world's first charter of human rights. Passages in this appear to express Cyrus' respect for humanity and his promotion of religious tolerance and freedom, and his support for freedom of local religions and opposition to slavery, repression and tyranny.

> I am Cyrus, king of the world, great king, legitimate king, king of Babylon ... I did not allow anybody to terrorize [any place] of the [country of Sumer] and Akkad. I strove for peace in Babylon and in all his [other] sacred cities. As to the inhabitants of Babylon ... I abolished forced labour ... I returned to these sacred cities ... the images which [used] to live therein and established for them permanent sanctuaries. (quoted by Michalowski, 2006, p426-30)

But these achievements were dismissed in the Greek accounts of the Persians that followed the war. Herodotus, born four years before the final conflict, became the victors' historian. In his account of the history of the world he knew *The Histories* (1972), his early use of the word *barbaroi* did not carry the connotations of the modern day barbarian. In the initial chapters it was not a pejorative term, nor was it used to distinguish easterners from westerners. But in the later books that focus on the events of 480 BCE, Herodotus uses *barbaroi* as a term of vilification: as the forces of Xerxes are introduced, they become the barbarians, tyrants, leading a despotic superstate against the gallant little Greek democratic communities: it is an initial run of the battle of 'freedom' against the 'axis of evil' –

> history's original villains, ... the Orientals against whom the first European civilisation defined itself. ... In winning their nationhood, the Greeks consigned the Persians to a miserable place in the world's memory. (Jones, 2005)

Herodotus wrote 40 years after the events: a more contemporary view on the Persians is given by the playwright Aeschylus, who fought at the battle of Marathon. His play *The Persians*, written just ten years after the events, gives voice to the idea of 'the Glorious West', in opposition to the East, the seat of slavery, brutality and ignorance. The Queen of Persia in the Persian royal palace at Susa receives news of the defeat of her son Xerxes.

> Queen: Who commands [the Hellenes]? Who is shepherd to their host?
>
> Chorus: They are slaves to none, neither are thy subjects. No longer will they that dwell throughout the length and breadth of Asia abide under the Persian yoke, nor will they pay further tribute through the master's crushing necessity, nor will they fall headlong on the ground to revere him, since the kingly power has utterly perished. Aeschylus: The *Persians* (Vellacott, 1961, lines 585-90)

As Norman Davies puts it, Aeschylus

> creates a lasting stereotype, whereby the civilized Persians are reduced to cringing, ostentatious, arrogant, cruel, effeminate, and lawless aliens. Henceforth, all outsiders stood to be denigrated as barbarous. No one could compare to the wise, courageous, judicious and freedom-loving Greeks. (Davies, 1996, p103)

Greece is all liberty, Persia all tyranny. Edith Hall shows how the Athenian playwrights of the period used images of incest, polygamys murder, sacrilege, impalement, castration, female power, and despotism to define the non-Greek world. The playwrights conceptualised the barbarian as the negative embodiment of Athenian civic ideals. These invented barbarians became a powerful cultural expression of Greek xenophobia and chauvinism (Hall, 1989). The Greeks divided the world between themselves and the barbarians: Asiatic barbarians were described as servile, with no pride, simply slaves. The disdain of barbarians is directed at their intrinsic nature as human beings.

This complex of superiority was adopted in large part by the Romans – although they did allow that barbarians could, by due diligence, fealty and deeds, attain Roman citizenship. The concept of otherness, of the outsider – and of orientalism, a disdain for the east, pervaded first Greek, then Roman, and then European senses of identity.

> In this particular encounter began the idea of 'Europe', with all its arrogance, all its implications of superiority, all its assumptions of priority and antiquity, all its pretensions to a natural right to dominate. (Ascherson, 1995, p49)

Throughout subsequent centuries, Western writers and artists have repeatedly represented this military conflict as a triumph of Western ideals of freedom and self-determination over the slavish submission to repressive forces of oriental despotism. Thus Montaigne writes 'there are triumphant defeats that rival victories. Nor did those four sister victories, the fairest that the sun ever set eyes on-Salamis, Plataea, Mycale, and Sicily – ever dare match all their combined glory against the glory of the annihilation of King Leonidas and his men at the pass of Thermopylae' (Montaigne, 1965, p157).

Hegel opined that: '[The Persian Wars] live immortal not in the historical records of Nations only, but also of Science and of Art – of the Noble and the Moral generally. For these are World-Historical Victories; they were the salvation of culture and spiritual vigour and they rendered the Asiatic principle powerless' (Hegel, 2007, p257).

John Stuart Mill suggested that

> The battle of Marathon, even as an event in English history, is more important than the battle of Hastings. If the issue of that day had been different, the Britons and the Saxons might still have been wandering in the woods. (Mill, quoted in Murray, 1970, p461)

The creation of this first European identity includes ideas of other-ing, of boundaries and exclusion – and of xenophobia and the denigration of the illicit orient. These ideas suffused the Hellenic world and the Roman civilisation that followed. The European world and identity centred on the Mediterranean for many centuries, until the second major critical event. This was the reformulation and re-orientation of the European identity that started with the onset of the middle ages. Traditionally, historians have dated the Middle Ages from the fall of Rome and the Roman Empire early in the 5th century, a theory Edward Gibbon famously put forward in the 18th century (Gibbon, 1994/1776). By this time the Empire had split, and had two capitals – Rome and Constantinople – and the Alans, Goths, Huns and Visigoths, archetypal 'barbarians' in the discourse of the times, had been harrying the Roman forces for several decades. They laid siege to Rome and sacked the imperial city in 410, and then moved through France, settled in Aquitaine, then moved on again to Spain, along the North African coast till they conquered Carthage, the great Roman city port that accessed the wheat and oil of the North African territories.

The thesis that these events destroyed Roman-European culture and started 'the dark ages' has been seriously challenged by historians over the last 80 years (for example, Le Goff, 2005). They point to the essential continuity of the economy of the Roman Mediterranean long after the barbarian invasions, and show, with much archaeo-logical evidence (Hodges and Whitehouse, 1983), that the Roman way of doing things did not fundamentally change in the time im-mediately after the 'fall' of Rome. Barbarians came to Rome not to destroy it, but to take part in its benefits; they tried to preserve the Roman way of life.

The first and most prominent proponent of this thesis is the renowned Belgian historian, Henri Pirenne. *Mohammed and Charlemagne* (Pirenne, 1936) challenged the notion that Germanic barbarians had ended the Roman Empire. The trade routes across the Mediterranean remained essentially intact, and archaeological remains, particularly pottery and coins, and records of the time, show that Mediterranean goods continued to be traded across much of the territory of what had been the western empire: gold, fabrics, spices and papyrus (Hodges and Whitehouse, 1983). These goods did not disappear from western Europe till the 7th century. The migrant tribes preserved what political institutions they could, and did not deliberately destroy the classical civilisation. Germanic invaders made determined efforts to preserve classical culture, as did the church. Pirenne went on to analyse the impact of the Islamic expansions into North Africa, the eastern Mediterranean and Spain in the 7th and early 8th centuries: he concluded that it was the rise of Islam that overthrew the Roman mastery of the sea lanes, and it was this that detached the western empire from the eastern empire. Byzantium became cut off – and these dramatic changes isolated the Merovingian kings in north-west Europe. Between Mohammed's death in 632 and 732, Islam conquered first Syria, Persia, Palestine and Egypt, and then Kabul, Samarkand and Bokhara in the east, and Carthage and Tangier in the west. In 711 Islamic forces crossed to the Iberian peninsular and swept though Visigoth Spain so that just one hundred years after Mohammed's death they were at Tours, only 200 km from Paris. There, Charles Martel was able to lead forces into the Battle of Poitiers that halted their advance and they retreated to the Pyrenees. A great swathe of Muslim territory now cut Christian Europe off from direct contact with almost every other civilisation and religion.

The rupture of economic ties to Europe disconnected the continent from trade and turned it into a backwater, with wealth flowing out in the form of raw resources and nothing coming back. There was a steady decline, so that by the time of Charlemagne Europe had become entirely agrarian at a subsistence level, with no long-distance trade. This reorientation of Europe precipitated the establishment of the Carolingian empire, remote and isolated from the Mediterranean trade, and the Pope had to align himself with this new north eastern Europe in the late eighth century – to the extent that Charlemagne was crowned Emperor in Rome on Christmas Day 800. Pirenne concludes, in a famous passage:

> Without Islam, the Frankish Empire would have probably never existed. It is therefore strictly correct to say that without Mohammed, Charlemagne would have been inconceivable. (Pirienne, 1936, p234)

The new empire of the west became 'the scaffolding of the middle ages' (Davies, 1996, p256) and led to a major reorientation of European identity. Europe was turned in on itself – commercial, academic and political discourses were severed. While the beleaguered Byzantine eastern empire became heavily absorbed in defending its eastern frontiers, the west had to fend for itself, developing its own economy and autonomy: as Davies puts it, the spread of Islam

> ... gave a major impetus to feudalism ... it destroyed the supremacy which the Mediterranean lands had hitherto exercised over [all Europe]. Before Islam, the post-classical world of Greece and Rome ... had remained essentially intact. After Islam, it was gone for ever. Almost by default, the political initiative passed from the Mediterranean to the emerging kingdoms of the north... It created a cultural bulwark against which European identity could be defined. Europe, let alone Charlemagne, is inconceivable without Muhammad. (Davies, 1996, p257)

Instead of seeing the medieval period as the dark ages, some historians are now suggesting that the changes imposed by these events in the eighth century revitalised and redirected the creation of the European identity. In the empire of Charlemagne we see a new political entity emerging, a strong empire, specifically allied to the papacy, which took economic and political initiatives that would have been inconceivable earlier. In his court the term 'Europe' was revived, to describe the area he reigned over – an area that did not incorporate Byzantium, nor the Muslim lands to the south, nor the pagan lands to the north, nor all Christendom.

The Frankish Empire incorporated what is now western and central Europe, and Charlemagne is regarded by some as the founding father of both French and German monarchies, and as a father of Europe: his empire united most of western Europe for the first time since the Romans, and the Carolingian renaissance encouraged the formation of a common European identity. His reinstatement in Rome of an evicted and weakened Pope was reciprocated when the Pope crowned him Emperor, thus usurping the place of the Emperor in Constantinople. Charlemagne tackled the problems of the lack of access to gold, brought about by the Islamic expansion, with a re-configuration based on a silver currency, soon adopted beyond his own territories, a strategy that economically harmonised and unified the complexity of currencies that has been in use, simplifying trade and commerce. Prices were controlled; taxes on particular goods raised revenue for government. The contacts with the culture and learning of other European areas – Visigothic Spain, Anglo-Saxon England and Lombard Italy soon led to the establishment of monastic schools and centres for book-copying: many surviving works of classical Latin were copied and preserved by Carolingian scholars.

What were the characteristic features of the identity of Europe in the middle medieval period that began with the consolidation of Islam and the foundation, in reaction, of the Carolingian regime? One was the consolidation and spread of Latin Christianity. The expansion of the church was marked by the establishment of new bishoprics that both pushed back the territory of Moorish Spain, and expanded into the Scandinavian and Baltic areas. Latin Christendom made

> the images of exclusion and otherness available to those who formed and expressed opinions in twelfth century western Europe .. [these] included not only the dichotomy Christian/non Christian, but also that of civilised/barbarian, and the two polarities were often mutually reinforcing. (Bartlett 1994, 24)

The Welsh were 'rude and untamed': they 'nominally profess Christ but deny him in their life and customs' (Millor *et al*, 1986). The Ruthenians 'confess Christ only in name, but deny him in their deeds': they were 'primitive Slavs and wild peoples' (Appelt and Irgang, 1963).

Coupled with this was the establishment of new trading routes within Europe, focusing on the major north and west flowing rivers, and the North Sea, the Baltic and the Irish Sea. These were sufficiently strong to incorporate and Christianise the Viking incursions, and to rapidly adopt the settlement patterns and political structures of Frankish Europe. Thereafter, western Europe adopted a colonial pattern that followed both trade and the church, and there were numerous examples of western Europeans establishing trading colonies across northern and eastern Europe – in Riga, for example.

Historians sometimes refer to the Europeanisation of Europe in the tenth to twelfth centuries: they refer to the spread of the construct of Europe into areas beyond the Frankish heartlands. This was not simply by military conquest, although there were series of military expansions outwards from the core. It was also cultural: the Hungarian historian Fügedi (1975, p494) writes 'we maintain that Hungary was Europeanised in the course of the twelfth and thirteenth centuries', while in Leon and Castile the ruler Alfonso V1 has been described as 'anxious to Europeanise his realm' and to 'Europeanise the liturgy' (Lomax, 1978, p56).

This aculturation was manifest in the way that that people's forenames changed: local names were replaced by the adoption of western Christian names in the younger generations; saints' names in local churches were replaced by saints' names of the Latin cannon. Another important integrative element was the University – 'one of the most powerful instruments of cultural homogeneity to arise in the High Middle Ages' (Bartlett, 1994, p288). From the core of France and northern Italy in the late eleventh century, the idea of the University spread with the development of the European area – from the original golden triangle, to middle Europe, Scotland and Scandinavia, and as far as Istanbul.

The effects of Charlemagne – and of Mohammed – as Bartlett wrote, were that:

by 1300 Europe existed as an identifiable cultural entity. It could be described in more ways than one, but some common features of its cultural face are the saints, names, coins, charters and educational practices ... Europe's names and cults were more uniform than they had ever been, Europe's rulers everywhere minted coins and depended on chanceries; Europe's bureaucrats shared a common experience of higher education. This is the Europeanization of Europe. (Bartlett, 1994, p291)

From this period on, European mariners were able to land armies at any point in the known world (though the military might of the armies was not always so pre-eminent as that of the mariners). The Germans, abetted by Danes and Swedes, made the Baltic a Catholic lake. Italian and Hanseatic merchants stretched around in a pincer movement, meeting in the Ukraine. The trading cities of Hamburg, Lubeck, Genoa and Venice expanded and integrated the economy and culture of Europe. But the 'others' that the Europeans encountered in these ventures were very different.

To the south, they were confronted with societies at least as wealthy, populous, urbanised and literate as Latin Christendom, in the Muslim and the Orthodox spheres. They might have abhorrent religious beliefs – but they were monotheistic religions, based on truths revealed through scripture. But to the north and east the other was less populous, rural, non-literate, with polytheistic, local and idolatrous religions. These peoples could be converted, or westernised, or otherwise incorporated in a way that the societies to the south could not. The Slav rulers could also see what they could gain by being incorporated into the west. The development of attitudes that lead to expectations of colonial domination and expansion came from this northern and north-eastern orientation, rather than from the south. Colonisation was the reproduction of the social frameworks of the homeland, rather than subordination: the spread 'by a kind of cellular multiplication' (Bartlett, 1994, 391) of the cultural and social forms of the Latin Christian core. Adoption of Christianity signified loyalty, and brought with it freedoms, liberties and inclusion – but the Christianity was non-negotiable.

To the south, Muslim communities were given rights in much the same was as Jews were – their religion was, within certain limits, guaranteed and accepted. In the north, the choice between resistance and conversion was sharp: in the south, there was a third possibility, of continuing as a defeated but tolerated minority. Mediaeval Europe generated institutional and attitudinal racism as part of its colonial dispositions. This new European identity profoundly influenced the Europeans who followed – but the Europeans of the sixteenth century, at the beginning of the modern era, were also shaped by a new set of factors,

The third critical moment is epitomised by the fall of Constantinople in 1453. The attacking forces of Ottomans (and others) led by the young sultan, Mehmed II, met the defenders, a motley group of Byzantine Greeks and others, led by Constantine XI Palaiologos, the last Emperor. The fall of Constantinople was of only symbolic significance: it had long become a cultural backwater in Europe. Some of the Byzantines themselves were not minded to associate with the Latin west. The Byzantium Admiral, Lucas Notaras, although active in the defence of the city, was recorded as remarking that he would 'sooner [be subject to] the Sultan's Turban than the Papal Tiara' (Herrin, 2007) – an interesting example of 'othering' that was heard reflected in an English football fan's chant in 2007, just before a match against Scotland – 'I'd sooner wear a turban than a kilt'.

Before and immediately after the conquest of Mehmed, many of the materials and documents of Constantinople were finding their way to western Europe: most important were the Greek texts that became the foundation of the renaissance that had started in northern Italy in the fourteenth century. This received a significant boost with the fall of Constantinople. Renaissance scholars sought out ancient texts, typically written in Latin or ancient Greek, scouring monastic libraries for works of antiquity that fallen into obscurity. They wanted to improve and perfect their worldly knowledge; a radically different approach to the transcendental spirituality of medieval Christianity. It was not a rejection of Christianity, but a subtle shift in the way that intellectuals approached religion, reflected in many other areas of cultural life. Thus artists tried to portray the human form realistically, developing ways of showing perspective and light; political philosophers such as Machiavelli tried to describe political life as it really was, and to improve government on the basis of rationality. As well as using classical Latin and Greek, writers increasingly used vernacular languages; and this with the invention of moveable typeface allowed many more people access to print.

The Renaissance was a rebirth of classical ideas lost to western Europe, fuelled by the rediscovery of ancient texts from the Eastern Roman Empire and the Islamic world, and the translations of Greek and Arabic texts into Latin. Greek and Arabic knowledge was assimilated from Spain and also directly from the Greek and Arab-speaking world. Mathematics flourished in the Middle East, and mathematical knowledge was brought back by crusaders after 1204 – and the final fall of Constantinople brought a sharp increase in the exodus of Greek scholars, bringing with them texts and knowledge.

The Renaissance sparked off a remarkable reconfiguration in Europe. Ross (2004) refers to the parallel events between five hundred years ago and the present, in terms of redefining social relationships. Schultze (2004) points to the striking similarity between the descriptions used in the early 21st century and those used by people in the sixteenth century when confronted with the loss of certainty in the early modern period. The series of loosely-linked events triggered by the renaissance led to another reconfiguration of the identities of Europeans. One of these – the development of humanism, exemplified by the work of Erasmus – was and remains a key element of European identity: a shift from the theocratic world-view of the medieval population to an anthropocentric view. There were many others. The work of Copernicus and those who followed him challenged the geocentric view of the Greek and Roman writers that had been adopted as the new orthodoxy of the Latin church and its rulers. But the renaissance also led to the 'age of exploration'. This not only allowed the first complete view of the relationship of all parts of the earth, so that Europe began to realise that the world was more than Europe, but also allowed Europe to unleash its characteristic colonialism on the rest of the world.

38

These new 'others', 'discovered' by the voyages of exploration, were even more heathen and more barbarian than the north Europeans, and many resisted the idea that they should adopt the culture of the Europeans. The emerging European technology of firearms – exemplified by Mehmed II's employment of Hungarian cannon to attack the walls of Constantinople – represented a burgeoning European arms industry that helped the colonial conquests. The development of the musket made for a new mass-produced weapon, highly portable, that could be used to kill large numbers at a much greater distance than had been possible with conventional weaponry. The final stage of the *reconquista* of the Iberian peninsular was marked by far less accommodating attitudes towards the Muslims of Spain and Portugal. The expulsion of the Moors from Granada in Spain after some 800 years of settlement there began ethnic cleansing policies that are still found in Europe. Muslims were required to convert or leave, and this policy was then applied to the Jews of Spain, and then the Jews of Portugal. Religious 'acts of faith' – *autos-da-fe* – became fires that burned to preserve the purity of the blood.

Technology was evident also in mass communication: Gutenberg efficiently exploited moveable typeface using the roman alphabet from about 1450 in Mainz. The books of the ancient world, as well as the Bible, became much more available to Europeans of a wide range of social classes and languages. This new technology, linked to the new questioning nature of the age, led to the reformation, and in turn to the great European wars of the fifteenth and early sixteenth centuries. The Peace of Ausberg in 1555 effectively recognised the fragmentation of Europe with the principle that each rule had the right to determine the religion of his own state and the people who lived in it – Catholicism, Lutheranism or Calvinism (*cuius regio, eius religio*). The nation state had become part of the European identity. The Peace of Westphalia (1648), the first modern diplomatic congress, initiated a new order based on the concept of national sovereignty and territorial integrity. The interests and goals of nation states were now assumed to transcend those of any individual citizen or even any ruler, and the Westphalian doctrine of states as independent actors bolstered the rise of 19th century nationalism.

Legitimate states were assumed to correspond to *nations* – groups of people united by language and culture – or, as Benedict Anderson says, 'imagined communities' (1983).

The fall of Constantinople triggered the Renaissance, the Reformation and the rise of the autonomous nation state. Within the span of a single lifetime revolutionary changes began in society, knowledge and government which marked the birth of the modern era and the transition point from medievalism. European identity now had not just a new humanist streak, but also a new nationalistic streak. The colonial identity of medieval Europe was augmented by a fearful technology, with the power to export this mix to the world. This led to the series of events between 1914 and 1945 that marked the end-point of the mix of identities that characterised the growth of Europe. Seeing the other as barbarian, cultural imperialism, colonialism, nationalism: these characteristics of European identity culminated in an orgy of destruction and bloodletting that far eclipsed previous massacres.

Jean Monnet, as a member of the French government in exile, declared in August 1943:

> There will be no peace in Europe, if the states are reconstituted on the basis of national sovereignty... The countries of Europe are too small to guarantee their peoples the necessary prosperity and social development. The European states must constitute themselves into a federation... (Monnet, 1976, p222)

Nation states were a problem. Ernest Renan's lecture on 'What is a nation?' (Renan, 1882) was the forerunner of the more widespread acknowledgement that the Westphalian system that had been born of and shaped Europe was outdated. In 1998 the NATO Secretary General Javier Solana observed:

> the Westphalian system had its limits. For one, the principle of sovereignty it relied on also produced the basis for rivalry, not community of states; exclusion, not integration. ... Humanity and democracy: two principles essentially irrelevant to the original Westphalian order. (Solana, 1998)

The German Foreign Minister Joschka Fischer pointed out that the system was obsolete:

> the core of the concept of Europe after 1945 was and still is a rejection of the European balance-of-power principle and the hegemonic ambitions of individual states that had emerged following the Peace of Westphalia in 1648, a rejection which took the form of closer meshing of vital interests and the transfer of nation-state sovereign rights to supranational European institutions (Fischer, 2000)

So what are the identifying characteristics of Europe today? European society is characterised by its social and cultural diversity, which gives us great strength but also presents challenges. European society can be seen moving towards a belief in equality, linked to a desire to challenge and counter inequalities, to promote social cohesion, and to work for distributive justice. But diversity also means that there are inequalities and disadvantaged groups – socially, economically and culturally – and Europe is, to some extent, addressing these inequalities whilst also preserving its diversity. European social values are not in themselves unique and are shared by some other nations and regions of the world. But they are nevertheless a particular combination, articulated in a distinctive way. They also have a degree of fragility and need to be defended and extended, and we sometimes need to be better at putting them into practice. There are five particular areas in which European identity is distinct and positive – though within each there are practices that need to be improved, challenged and extended (Ross, in Isaacs, 2008, p44-47). These will be expanded on in chapter six: in brief , Europe today is founded on:

- essential and legal enshrined human rights

- a broadly common idea of social welfare and of the role of the state in this, and a shared belief that the disadvantaged are not to be blamed for their own misfortune, and that society has the collective responsibility to care for them

- education based on principles of free and universal access, with an open attitude towards knowledge, helping individuals to achieve both vertical and horizontal mobility

■ increased levels of mobility, for study, employment and for leisure, breaking down barriers, decreasing scepticism and broadening views about the cultural values of others

■ an attitude towards language and communication that seeks to preserve linguistic diversity and to improve understanding and appreciation of diversity

Our ability to learn from each other is a major and new characteristic of European identity, and our diversity is a very positive aspect of this. Beck points out that: 'The 'we' who legitimise the cosmopolitan legal regime are the *prospective* Europeans who in this way become the subject of their own history' (Beck and Grande, 2007, p8, emphasis as in original). We have learned from our history, and we are learning to trust each other, to be reflective, and to use best practice. We share all kinds of knowledge and ways of thinking and Europe generally is willing to negotiate, discuss and compromise on settling problems and issues. Our diversity means that we have many models to observe and to learn from. Beck says: 'what is lacking is not a single European identity that unites everyone, but a narrative of Europeanization that makes sense of the interrelations between new departures and declines' (Beck and Grande, 2007, p4).

These new identity markers for Europe have developed over the past sixty years, and are of a distinctly different character to what went before. And this appears to be the very heart of European identities today: we are not the past. Europe is now based on identifying a new kind of 'other': our own past. We do not identify ourselves with nor carry out the practices of the generations before us. This is not simply a negative rejection of the past, but a positive affirmation of these values. The past is another country: they did things differently there.

This imposes a particular burden on education: the generations that can recall the old Europe, the Europe that we have rejected, is dying out, and educators must ensure that we keep alive that fierce understanding of the need to move away from the old identities. The forms of citizenship needed to do this must take on an active form, rather than passive acceptance, and we now turn to the distinction between education for active citizenship and for passive citizenship.

4

Education for Active and Passive Citizenship

C hapter two introduced some considerations of the nature and purposes of citizenship education, and in particular of its relationship to models of education and its place in the curriculum. But there are different forms and kinds of citizenship education, often instigated with different motives and with varied planned objectives. This is as true in the European context as it is in national educational systems. This chapter examines some of the rationales and expectations behind these, and distinguishes two potential kinds of citizenship: the active and the passive. Active citizenship should be encouraged and developed by educators (even though this might not necessarily be the first choice of all policy makers) and the context of contemporary Europe makes the development of an active citizenry particularly necessary.

Why have politicians and policy makers, both in individual countries and in the European arena, sought to introduce citizenship education with spirited and enthusiastic initiatives over the past ten years? What are the implications for teachers of the various models held by politicians and policy makers, and how are teachers expected to introduce possibly contentious issues into their teaching?

Citizenship education is being initiated in many countries in Europe, from England in 1999 to Spain and Greece in 2007, as well as in the European Union. These schemes and proposals come at a time when there is a decline in understanding, sympathy and trust in politicians and political institutions. For example, in the UK elections of 2001

Table 4.1: European Parliament Elections: Voter Turnout across the EU (1979-2004) (%)

	1979	1984	1989	1994	1999	2004
Austria	-	-	-	67.7 (1996)	49.0	41.8
Belgium*	91.6	92.2	90.7	90.7	90.0	90.8
Denmark	47.1	52.3	46.1	52.9	50.4	47.8
Finland	-	-	-	60.3 (1996)	30.1	41.1
France	60.7	56.7	48.7	52.7	47.0	43.1
Germany	65.7	56.8	62.4	60	45.2	43.0
Greece *	78.6 (1981)	77.2	79.9	71.2	70.2	62.8
Ireland	63.6	47.6	68.3	44	50.5	59.7
Italy	85.5	83.9	81.5	74.8	70.8	73.1
Luxembourg *	88.9	87	87.4	88.5	85.8	90.0
Netherlands	57.8	50.5	47.2	36	29.9	39.1
Portugal	-	72.2 (1987)	51.1	35.5	40.4	38.7
Sweden	-	-	-	41.6 (1995)	38.3	45.9
Spain	-	68.9 (1987)	54.8	59.1	64.4	37.2
UK	31.6	32.6	36.2	36.4	24.0	38.9
Cyprus						71.2
Czech Republic						27.9
Estonia						26.9
Hungary						38.5
Latvia						41.2
Lithuania						48.2
Malta						82.4
Poland						20.4
Slovakia						16.7
Slovenia						28.3

* voting compulsory

Source: *European Parliament Elections 2004: results* (Euractive, 2004)

and 2005 there was a declining voter turnout (Electoral Commission, 2005). In most European Union countries the 1999 and 2004 elections to the European Parliamentary elections showed a low and falling participation rate, as is shown in Table 4.1.

Younger voters appear to be even less inclined to turn out to vote than older generations. The traditional explanation for this offered by many politicians and policy makers is that they have not had sufficient, if any, citizenship or political education (Bromley *et al*, 2004). This argument suggests that schools have let down their respective counties: if schools had been successful in teaching pupils about the virtues of democracy, young people would be motivated to participate in elections. The politicians need to achieve substantial popular endorsement at the polls, or else they will lack the authority and legitimacy to govern. The political system, not just the governing party, requires a political mandate that demonstrates that the majority of the population believes in and accepts the governmental and political systems that they stand for. The need for legitimacy is the principal motivation.

The gap between the total electorate and the numbers who vote is sometimes referred to as a 'democratic deficit' (Moravsci, 2004): the desire to narrow this is a powerful stimulus for the current political emphasis on programmes for citizenship. A considerable literature has developed on this democratic deficit in a number of countries in the world (see, for example, Verdun, 1998; Moravsci, 2004; Avbelj, 2005; Mitchell, 2005; Hirschhorn, 2006). Membership of political parties in many parts of the world is declining and younger people, it is claimed – if they are interested in politics at all – are subscribing to 'single issue' political groups, around, for example, environmental concerns or global poverty. Much of the policy pressure for developing citizenship education has come from this source: politicians and political structures derive their power to act from the fact that a high proportion of the electorate have subscribed to their election. Similar arguments are found across the European Union: the legitimacy of the European parliament is questionable if it is only elected by a small fraction of the population and its authority can be restored by greater political participation in the elections, and it is sometimes argued that this can only be achieved by teaching the virtues of electoral democracy. Political education is being introduced, at least in part, to address a political problem of democratic deficit, which may be a controversial issue in itself.

There are also controversial elements in the conceptions of democracy and citizenship. Citizenship 'for democracy' is particularly problematic: as Borhaug (1999) points out, it depends on what kind of democracy. Traditional representative democracy simply ensures intermittent participation in elections, through political parties that stand for broad principles. The key actor in this is the informed voter. Citizens are needed in order to show their support for the system through the ballot box: they need to understand how to do this, and why this is necessary, and to gather the information necessary to exercise some form of choice – but no more than this.

The classic 1960s study of political sociology, *The Civic Culture*, suggested that the ideal citizen was a careful mix of the active citizen and the passive subject (Almond and Verba, 1965). The citizen was an active voter, even an active member of a political party, but was passive in accepting the system, in accommodating the compromises inherent in mass political party politics, and in tolerating the political candidates and policies put up for public discussion and election. But there are other kinds of democratic action, and many people over the past two decades have become involved in more focused political activities, rather than supporting mainstream political parties. The growth of what is sometimes called single issue politics has challenged traditional politicians, who have found electors – and young people in particular – deserting mass parties in favour of pressure groups, such as, in the UK, Drop the Debt, Comic Relief, Make Poverty History and coalitions of Greens (Holden, 2006). The old political parties have had their activities and compromises challenged by informed political activists. This alternative democracy is less concerned with the political structures and procedures than with the issues themselves. The key actor becomes the local activist.

This outcome of political activism is not necessarily what politicians and public servants want, nor what they would like citizenship education to be concerned with. Their principal concerns in this area are, quite understandably, with buttressing the systems and institutions that brought them into existence and that maintain them. This is also about civic duties and obligations – to participate in political processes, to understand the need for compromise, to accept the decision-making processes. From their perspective, future citizens need to understand the fairness of the existing system, and to accept its long historical antecedents. It is remarkable how many European countries, from Iceland to Greece, claim to have the oldest, or one of the oldest, democratic or parliamentary systems in the world! Young people, it is claimed, need to understand and appreciate how the machinery of government works in the interest of the citizen, how interest groups must of course be listened to, but that balances must be struck between competing interests – then they will accept the legitimacy of the political processes, and become part of *The Civic Culture* – the good citizen.

However, there are other arguments for citizenship education, and other models of what constitutes good citizenship practice. Many of those involved in the citizenship education movement seek to develop educational processes that empower active citizens. By this they mean individuals who are able to critically engage with, and seek to affect the course of, social events. To paraphrase the distinction, active citizenship can be seen as being about doing things, while passive citizenship is simply about the status or act of being a citizen. This distinction between active and passive citizenship has been particularly discussed and debated over the past five years (Ireland *et al*, 2006; Nelson and Kerr, 2006) and there is as yet no international consensus or agreement on terms. A model that has been recently suggested by Kennedy (2006) may be helpful in clarifying some of the issues involved in categorising various forms of activity and passivity in citizenship.

Kennedy distinguished four forms or levels of activity in citizenship. The first of these is what may be termed conventional political activity. This is activity at the level at which those concerned with the democratic deficit would have us act, such as engaging in voting, in belonging to a political party, and in standing for office. Voting, though an activity, is rather a minimalist action. But nevertheless, these kinds of traditional conformist activities are a form of active participation, and they are a form that has the intention to effect change in civic society.

The second form of citizenship activity lies in participating in social movements and in being involved with voluntary activities. This may be either working as a volunteer with charities and social agencies, or perhaps collecting money on their behalf. This form of participation in civil society (as opposed to the former civic action) is essentially conformist and ameliorative in nature. The activities are designed to repair problems, rather than to address causes, or even to acknowledge possible causes. In this form of action there is no necessity to be concerned with addressing any underlying political or socio-economic trends or activities that may be creating the social problem that is being addressed. The concept of 'service education', which is particularly prevalent in the United States, falls into this category.

These first two forms of active citizenship – conventional political participation and social volunteering – constitute what is sometimes derided as the 'voting and volunteering' approach to citizenship education.

The third form of active citizenship is action for social change, in which the individual is involved in activities that aim to change political and social policies. These forms of activity might range from activities such as letter writing and signing petitions to working with pressure groups and participating in demonstrations, pressure groups and other ways of trying to influence decision making. These political activities often tend to focus around a particular cause – such as climate change, nuclear weapons, animal rights, poverty or homelessness. Social volunteering may also often be 'single issue' in its scope, but the distinction between this and political change is that those involved in volunteering seek primarily or only to make amends for and to restore the outcomes of perceived inequity, while those participating in political change intend to address and change the root causes of inequalities or injustices. This form of active citizenship also includes a range of various illegal variants, such as taking part in occupations, writing graffiti or other forms of civil disobedience. Common to both legal and non-legal forms of activity is a conflictual model of civic and civil change.

Kennedy's fourth active form – which it might be argued is, for a variety of socio-cultural reasons, particular to the USA, the UK and the old Commonwealth – is enterprise citizenship. This is very much an individualistic model of citizenship action, in which the individual engages in a variety of such self-regulating activities as achieving financial independence, becoming a self-directed learner, being a problem solver and developing entrepreneurial ideas. This is very much an economic model of citizenship activity, and individualistic in its range. It is important to distinguish this idea of the economic individual from economic identity, in which an individual associates themselves with an economic group, such as users of a particular currency, or other social interactions that have an economic basis. Economic identities will be discussed in a subsequent chapter (see also Hutchings, Fulop and Van den dries, 2002).

It should be emphasised that these four forms in no sense constitute a hierarchy or sequential form of development – the individual does not need to progress through one form to achieve the next. Any curriculum should see these as potentially concurrent activities, any combination of which might be encouraged at any age or stage of development.

Kennedy also distinguished two form of passive citizenship. The first of these is concerned with national identity, where the individual understands and values the nation's history, and the symbolic and iconic forms of the nation – in its institutions, flag, anthem and political offices. This kind of passive citizenship is commonly taught through transmission models of education, through civic education and the hidden curriculum of unspoken mores, structures and assumptions. Many of the traditional markers of civic enculturation and learning, referred to in more detail in chapter ten below, are focused on measuring young people's abilities to recognise these iconic and symbolic forms of government and citizenship.

A second and variant form of passive citizenship is described by Kennedy as patriotism, a more extreme national identity that would include giving military service and offering unconditional support for one's country against any claims of other countries. This form of passive citizenship would inculcate values of loyalty, and unswerving obedience, and stress the value of social stability and hard work. Sheehan has pointed out that in Europe in the 19th century and the first half of the 20th century 'the duty to fight and perhaps die for the state was the (male) citizens' sacred obligation' (Sheehan, 2008, p179). This understanding of citizenship is now uncommon in most parts of Europe.

But these distinctions are not necessarily clear-cut, and certainly not exclusive. An analysis using this typology was made by Nelson and Kerr (2006), and this demonstrated that there are strong cultural variations in what might be considered as appropriate forms of 'active' citizenship in different countries. In some countries it is clearly considered that many of the attributes that are characterised by Kennedy as forms of passive citizenship are concerned with the accepting of the individual's status as a citizen, and these are perceived in those particular cultures as elements of active citizenship that are to be encouraged and developed. These variations almost certainly depend on the particular historical development and configuration of the state. In some countries, perhaps particularly in Europe, there is a stronger perception that citizenship and national identity, which will be considered in a subsequent chapter, may now be more usefully seen as social constructs, and that active citizenship may embrace a diverse range of relevant political scenarios in which to be a politically active citizen.

These analyses of citizenship, and the categorisations of active and passive citizenship, are concerned primarily with the relationship between the individual and the community: they encompass the extent of the obligation the individual has to participate in civic affairs. In this context, civic affairs may include a wide variety and levels of socio-political communities – local as well as national, regional and at times trans-national, and might include memberships of associations. Citizenship with this meaning thus takes in the extent to which the individual contributes to and participates in local affairs as well as national governance, and her or his involvement in decision making about how a social or political entity works. This sense of citizenship strongly implies the individual working towards the betterment of the communities that she or he lives in, whether it be through participating in decision making, voting, volunteer work, lobbying and campaigning, or other efforts to improve life for all citizens. The individual might, therefore, have different levels of activity and engagement in different levels of government – perhaps voting in national elections, but not European elections or local elections; actively lobbying local government institutions on issues, even on issues of a global nature, but not doing so at national government level. Multiple citizenship clearly is unproblematic in this concept of citizenship.

Citizenship has another level of meaning, however, as a legal status concerned with identification and allegiance to a particular state. This often brings with it a national identity, and specific legal obligations, duties and allegiance to a nation state. The traditional citizenship of modern times (approximately post-1500 CE, as discussed in the previous chapter) has been singular and exclusive, and has been acquired, depending on the specific national context, either by descent (*jus sanguinis* – by the law of blood or, as it would now be put, genetically), or by the place of birth (*jus solis* – by the law of the soil). When there were relatively low levels of international travel and settlement, complications and ambiguities were relatively few, and could be resolved by parental and community decisions. The increased level of international migration and settlement – and the relative ease of its being reversed – have led to the innovation of dual nationality, where an individual can hold full nationality of more than one state, sometimes until an age at which a choice must be made, sometimes for life, with dual obligations and rights. Multiple formal citizenship is therefore now possible. Moreover, formally and in law, those who are citizens of states in the European Community are citizens of both their own individual nation-states and citizens of Europe. Multiple legal citizenship has thus been possible for the past half century, and discussion about nested citizenship has been developed (for example, in Heater, 1990; European Union, 1992, 1993; and the Council of Europe, 2002).

The variant forms of levels of citizenship activity all imply a much greater sense of involvement in civic affairs than the passive acceptance of a legal status. In the specific European context, the possibilities for acting collaboratively on a cross-national or cross-cultural stage are potentially enhanced. The European context offers a forum for civic action that possesses real powers, as opposed to the exhortatory and *ad hoc* actions of international bodies such as the United Nations. Thus Davies and Issitt (2005) suggest that aspects of the global citizenship education programme might usefully be incorporated into citizenship education, as separation of global education from citizenship education appears to constrain both movements. Active citizenship, it is now suggested, will necessarily move beyond the confines of the nation state into contexts such as the European, and possibly global.

In an interesting meta-analysis, Bottery (2003) raises questions of political legitimacy and loyalty to the traditional state, in an era in which he points out is the very moment when the construction of nation states is being questioned. He sets out four potential future scenarios for citizenship education (p118-9): each of these constitute a form of active citizenship.

His first model is one in which nation states increase their control over education, and use education for specific utilitarian economic ends. In such a system curriculum content and assessment would be directed towards an intensified emphasis on the development of competences, particular employment-orientated competences. Educational policies would be geared towards the building of human resources in order to address economic competition, particularly in terms of national economies. In such a scenario, education for economic growth and full employment would also have the potential to

reduce civil discontent. Citizenship education would have a particular role in this process of reinforcing the legitimacy of these processes.

Bottery's second model is of a national system of citizenship education that was developed to reinforce intense commitment to particular beliefs based on the exclusion and fear of others, for example
in developing a specific ideological commitment to a particular
form of civilisation. The use of education to create a sense of othering is by no means new, and may be seen currently in many states
and nations, in a variety of cultures: it would by no means be found
only in non-western cultures.

Thirdly, citizenship education could help develop refined forms of
nested citizenship, in which the nation state is one of many different
levels of citizenship, with enhanced political participation at all
levels. Citizenship in this context would encourage learners to recognise the variety of political and social contexts in which they were
able to operate, and to understand which were most appropriate for
different political activities. An example of this is the way in which
the British electorate has elected Green Party members to the European Parliament and to the London Assembly but not to the UK

**Table 4.2 : Comparison of UK votes for selected parties,
European Parliamentary Election (2004) and UK National
Parliamentary Election (2005)**

Party	Europe, 2004		UK, 2005	
	Votes	%	Votes	%
Conservative	4,397,090	26.7	8,772,598	30.7
Labour	3,718,683	22.6	9,562,122	35.3
Liberal Democrat	2,452,327	14.9	5,981,874	22.1
UK Independence	2,650,768	16.1	603,298	2.2
Green	1,033,093	6.3	257,758	1.0
British National Party	808,200	4.9	192,746	0.7
Scottish National Party	231,505	1.4	412,267	1.5
Plaid Cymru	159,888	1.0	174,838	0.6

Source: *Interactive Results Service: UK Parliamentary general election, May 2005 results and
European Parliamentary election, June 2004* (Electoral Commission, 2008)

Parliament. European elections, despite the smaller turnout, have been seen by substantial numbers of electors as an appropriate forum in which to display their environmental concerns, while the same electors, in national elections, have chosen to vote along the socio-economic lines of the major UK parties.

Norman Davies, the author of *Europe: A history* (1996), points out that new forms of political organisation may be applicable. Instead of the sovereignty in which a state has sole authority over its citizens,

> it may be perfectly possible for people to recognise the authority of one government for one purpose and of other governments or agencies for other purposes. In some circumstances people could acquire the right to chose between competing jurisdictions in any given province or region. (Davies, 2007, p281)

He suggests that we may see multilayered multinational authorities, in which the principle of subsidiarity allows the delegation of

> decision making to the lowest and/or most appropriate level on each particular issue ... the best level may turn out to be far below or far removed from national government ... The world is being overtaken by a highly complex network of networks ... of interconnected and partially interlocking organisations. (p281-2)

Active citizenship in such scenarios will call for particularly informed and skilful citizens, but will also present many more forums for contributing to deliberative democracy, in which the citizen will be able to attain greater possibilities for participation and belonging.

This realisation that the nation state is no longer the only possible level of analysis – or even the most useful level – has been taken up by Ulrich Beck, writing with Edgar Grande in *Cosmopolitan Europe* (2007). Beck has elsewhere pointed out that

> social and political theory is, to some extent, still a prisoner of the nation-state. Most basic concepts of the social sciences -sociology, the state, democracy, community – are connected to the nation and to the nation-state form. This relates of course to the historical development of political thinking and of the social sciences – both acquired their modern form in the 19th century in the context of

imagining national communities. Most of the social sciences are still sticking to what I call the container model of society and politics. ... [But] we are living in an interconnected world in which the meaning of borders is changing ... We thus need new perspectives in order to understand contemporary interactions, decisions, institutions; we need transnational perspectives, or what I would call a cosmopolitan outlook.

The principle of cosmopolitanism is that all the possible cultural divergences have to be acknowledged as being different and equal at the same time. This means that differences are not neglected, but are valued as something productive, as important to self- definitions. ... we need a basic discussion about how far the recognition of the otherness of the other is acceptable or not acceptable to everybody. To acknowledge different cultures might be valued as long as these do not violate basic human rights. But, how to articulate these two statements is often a dilemma. (Beck, 2008, p8-9)

The fourth scenario for citizenship education set out by Bottery is one in which citizenship education simply becomes yet another consumer good, provided by one or other rival national or international organisations. This dystopia sees citizenship as a private product sold on the market by commercial educational providers, as the nation relinquishes its monopoly of educational provision.

Differentiating citizenship education into active and passive is controversial. For example, attempts to foster a passive form of citizenship at the national (Commonwealth) level in Australia have met some resistance (Prior, 2006), and there were still issues of moving between State and Commonwealth levels of citizenship identity, where Criddle et al (2004) noted a range of competing discourses. The development of citizenship as a simple passive identity has also led to issues where individuals are formally incorporated as citizens in France (Sutherland, 2002), while others identify similar concerns about identity and civic belonging amongst young people from non-German heritages in Germany (Mannitz, 2004a). In the next chapter we examine some of the practical educational strategies that might enable young people to become active citizens.

5
Practical Education for Active Citizenship

Some educators in contemporary Europe have approached the concept of European identity with some caution, suggesting that citizenship based on the new Europe needs to be distinctly different from the old citizenships of the nation-states: less ethnocentric, more diverse, more inclusive, and less wedded to nationalistic conceptions. Osler and Starkey (2003) have built on David Held's (1991, 1995) work on cosmpolitan democracy to advocate 'cosmopolitan citizenship', which they argue will prepare young people to live together in increasingly diverse local communities and an interdependent world. Beck's comments on cosmopolitanism in Europe, noted at the end of the last chapter, clearly relate to this. Hladnik (1995) argues that European citizenship should not be limited as a legal definition of status, and suggests that refugees also should be regarded as citizens, in a broad and inclusive definition, separate from historical definitions of citizenship by birth, ancestry or naturalisation. Various European Union programmes make much of the ideas of nested identities, and seek to promote citizenship at European level as part of a self-identity that includes national and regional elements.

What are the key elements of an active citizenship education programme? There is an emerging consensus (Crick and Lister, 1979; Crick, 1998; Kerr and Ireland, 2004; Cleaver and Nelson, 2006) that four elements can be distinguished in any effective citizenship education programme: values and dispositions, skills and competences, knowledge and understanding, and creativity and enterprise. The following paragraphs draw particularly on the UK experience of practice, with which I am most familiar, but the underlying principles will be of value in any European context.

First, and perhaps fundamental, is the identification and demonstration of certain values and dispositions, though the precise identification of these values, and the extent to which they are agreed to be universalistic, or even universalistic in contemporary times, is not unanimous. These key values might, for example, include the upholding of human rights (though, as will be discussed below, the conception of the extent of these rights continues to develop); ideas of social responsibility and obligations towards others, particularly in relation to equity, diversity and minorities; certain legal values, particularly those concerning the rule of law, democratic processes and various contested notions of freedom; and humanistic values of tolerance and empathy for others. This list may appear at first sight to be relatively uncontentious: a survey by Kidder (2002, in Sutherland, 2002) suggested that people from all across the world, when asked to identify their core moral values, would all agree on the same five ideas – honesty, respect, responsibility, fairness and compassion – but these words may have subtly different meanings or even less than subtle differences in different cultural contexts and societies.

Crick and Porter (1978) and Crick and Lister (1979), in their pioneering works on political literacy in the 1970s (described in Clarke, 2007), had a somewhat more critical edge on these values: they argue for attitudes of scepticism to be tempered with self-awareness, self-criticism and an awareness of consequence. They also qualified the conception of tolerance of the substantive values of other religious, ethical and political doctrines with the need to maintain particular procedural values necessary to freedom – respect for truth and reasoning, open-mindedness, and willingness to compromise. Toleration, they argued, was not just accepting difference, but welcoming diversity, though not exploitation, racism or the suppression of opinion. Memorably, having an open mind did not mean having an empty mind.

There was some early interest in political education in UK primary education in the late 1960s and 1970s as part of the political literacy movement of that time. Crick and Porter (1978) proposed that secondary pupils needed to become politically literate – developing the skills to evaluate political discussion and to make informed judgements between alternatives. Crick (1974) argued that his matrix of core concepts (figure 5.1) encompassed a far better reality of political activity than what he described as the sterile learning of structures.

These ideas were taken up by some teachers of younger children, and through the 1970s there were developments in primary school in political education, discussed later in this chapter. They included getting children to role-play decision-making about difficult situations on a deserted island, discussions of authority and power in local decisions, and drawing parallels between political and human politics. These activities were discreetly encouraged by official bodies at the time. In this way, some children became skilled at dealing with controversial or disputed subject matter albeit often through a make-believe world.

The 1980s were, in contrast, a period in which any form of teaching about society, let alone politics, was discouraged by the UK Government and its agents of curriculum development. The National Curriculum of 1988 only allowed the most traditional subjects, taught in a tightly controlled manner. Rather than foreground the democratic substance of citizenship, to make choices between different policies

Figure 5.1: Crick's matrix of core subjects

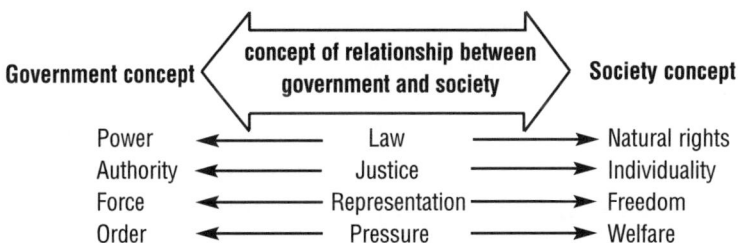

Source: derived from Crick (1974)

and agendas in electing their representatives, the emphasis was on the responsibilities that the citizen owed the state, exemplified in an influential book *The Principle of Duty* by David Selbourne (1994). Social education was downgraded as successive Ministers of Education promoted the core subjects, and left no place for learning about how society worked and the inevitable controversies within heterogeneous, multicultural communities (Ahier and Ross, 1994).

New Labour maintained many of the previous Government's policies including the structures of the curriculum. But a review of the National Curriculum and the subsequent Crick report led to the introduction of the new subject of Citizenship, formed around three strands: Social and moral responsibility, Community involvement and Political literacy. Citizenship education is now mandatory in secondary schools, and recommended in primary schools.

There have been parallel moves in the European Union. In *Towards a Europe of Knowledge* the former Commissioner for Education and Youth, Edith Cresson, called for

> the achievement of citizenship through the sharing of common values, and the development of a sense of belonging to a common social and cultural area ... a broader-base understanding of citizenship founded on mutual understanding of the cultural diversities that constitute Europe's originality and richness. (European Commission, 1997 p2)

There have also been initiatives designed to improve the understanding of European political institutions, calls for European citizenship, and to foster understanding of democracy amongst young people.

Planning how to locate these values within the curriculum raises particular issues. They cannot be introduced sequentially: there is no natural sequence of progression. I would argue that they need to be adopted in their entirety by every learning institution, and to inform the fundamental ethos of the institution. While the language used to articulate them will develop, the principles behind such a value as respect for individual rights, the rule of law, or acceptance of diversity should be as absolute and as manifest in the pre-school as they are in the university.

Thus Russell (2002) describes the theme of 'fairness' as central to the talk of seven and eight year-olds, and of eleven and twelve year-olds. His descriptions of practice with children of this age begin their discussions with broad definitions and refine these through interaction with others. 'Fair' is first defined as quantitative equity, and then expanded by the age of eleven to include forgiveness and reciprocity. As utilitarianism and deductive reasoning grow, girls tend to see fairness in terms of awareness of the needs of others and sharing, while boys move from fairness being keeping to the rules towards taking equity into account and accommodating individual difference. All the children in his study suggested doing what is 'right', even if this conflicted with authority.

But the ubiquity of these values does not imply that planning is not required: on the contrary, to articulate and live these values requires whole school planning of an exceptionally high order, moving from the didactic to the dialogic, so that all members of a school community understand and subscribe to them. It needs a constant programme of induction, so that new members of the school community (students, teachers, all non-teaching staff) are introduced to the practice of these values, and a continuing programme of self-critical questioning, to ensure the maintenance and possible extension of these values. What this entails will be discussed at greater length in chapter ten.

The second group of key elements comprise the skills and competences necessary to be a citizen. These include the skills of enquiry, of rationally seeking to establish processes, causes, and the bases for action; sophisticated skills of communication, which include being able to consider and respond to the views of others, being able to persuade, and being capable of being persuaded; skills of participation, which include an understanding of group dynamics and of how to contribute to the social development of civic action; and skills of social action.

These competences also need to be planned as part of the curriculum. While they need to be seen as all being in place throughout any educational institution, it is possible to consider and plan the progressive development of each of these skills. Communication skills, for example, will be developed through increasing levels of sophistication in listening and responding to others. This again raises important and fundamental questions for a school's learning style: teachers will need to model how to question, listen and respond in ways that are very different from traditional didactic models of teaching, dominated by simplistic models of transmission (Galton *et al,* 1980). To develop skills of communication in citizenship may require remodelling pedagogic styles in all subject areas, because switching from transmission-based teaching in mathematics to dialogic teaching in citizenship will be confusing and counterproductive for the learner.

Both these groups of key elements – values and skills – are necessary for active citizenship, as described in the previous chapter. The third group, of knowledge and understanding, are necessary, and sufficient, for passive citizenship, but also underpin active engagement. These include both a conceptual understanding of key concepts of politics and society, but also knowledge of particular institutions and their procedures, local, national and international. It can be argued that an understanding of the underlying principles of the role of the law, of the nature of representative democracy, the powers of and restraints on government, and some awareness of the premises of the economy, society and the environment are necessary for the educated citizen.

One can expect an increase in the depth of sophistication in the use of these conceptual terms over the educational cycle, and that some will develop a greater ability to discuss and articulate them. Schools could be reasonably expected to provide a *schema* for the introduction, development and assessment of these elements. Therein lies a particular danger: these items can be classified and assessed, while skills and values are far less susceptible to assessment and, as I have argued, should not be introduced sequentially, but all of a piece. Any emphasis on the measurement and categorisation of citizenship education might distort the curriculum to overemphasise these elements. Their assessment would enable a categorisation of the 'success' of individual pupils, teachers and schools, that would measure only a fraction of what needs to be accomplished in citizenship education, and would moreover be an assessment based on the one element alone that could lead to passive citizenship. Values, skills and knowledge are necessary factors for active citizenship, ineluctable, difficult to measure and imprecise though this may be; knowledge alone is sufficient for passive citizenship, though it may be efficiently and accurately assessed.

The final group of key elements have been defined (*inter alia* by Nelson and Kerr, 2006) as those attitudes that are concerned with creativity and enterprise, including ambition and being outward-looking in one's goals for learning and life. These are more individualistic elements, that for the sake of the argument of this chapter will be grouped alongside the values and attitudes of the first group.

This brings the argument back to the contemporary classroom. Teachers of pupils of all ages, including those teaching primary-aged children, are increasingly sure that children can understand political issues in a meaningful way, but there has been a dearth of research into this area since the initial groundbreaking studies by Greenstein (1965), Connell (1971) and Coles (1986). In the UK, Stevens suggested that seven year-olds 'have some cognitive contact with the political world': they saw political power as 'limited, consented to and conditional upon results' (1982, p38).

The work of teachers in the 1970s shows how pupils are able to develop political understanding. Margerison (1968, 1972) described an extended project, lasting several months, in which junior children developed an island society discussing the creation of social and political. Riches (1974) worked with 10 and 11 year-olds to develop a politically-focused programme based on the island theme, with discussion that made the links between the simulated activities and contemporary political processes explicit. Robins and Robins (1978) discussed a series of primary classroom activities that had a political focus. Wagstaff (1978) developed materials that encouraged the systematic examination of a series of eight social/political concepts through three environments that figured significantly in children's lives – the family, friendship groups and work. Ross (1981) used political fables (such Adams's *Watership Down* (1972), and Orwell's *Animal Farm* (1945) to draw parallels with human behaviour. Denscombe and Conway (1982) used issues in development education to examine a range of political concepts, using classroom discussion to explore questions around a conceptual framework. In these examples, the educator was in each case drawing on the children's experience of social life to identify examples of conflict and attempts at conflict resolution.

This approach has several common characteristics that are relevant for the contemporary classroom. It utilises the learners' experience, direct and vicarious, from role-playing, modelling, sharing stories, or watching the news. It uses discussion to get children to articulate their thoughts, and to construct meaning actively from the experience. By developing ideas in a social context with their peers (and with the teacher, and adults other than teachers) a shared understanding is achieved. The experience is around some particular issue, something that is possibly controversial, that arouses opinions, dissent and disagreement. Children are aware of dissent between adults, and the news media are increasingly able to bring 'breaking news' into the home and to the notice of the child. Issues of social justice (the treatment of suspected terrorism, or of asylum seekers), of environmental change (global warming, conservation, nuclear energy), and of war and peace (Iraq, Palestine, Sri Lanka ...) are put before children every day, and can evoke intense interests and passion. These are 'issues' *because* they are controversial, and it is *because* they are controversial that they are interesting to the child, and because they are controversial that it is important that future citizens learn how to understand them and how to take up defendable positions. It could be argued that it is the responsibility of the educational system to ensure that children develop strategies to understand, analyse, make decisions and argue beliefs around all these issues, in the same way and for the same reasons that schools help children understand fundamental science and how to learn to read. As the Crick report (1998) argued,

... at the immediate and practical level, it can be argued that controversial issues are important in themselves and to omit informing about and discussing them is to leave a wide and significant gap in the educational experience of young people, and is to fail to prepare them for adult life. Many controversial topics are major issues of the day: moral, economic, political and religious issues which young people ought to know about either because the issue could directly affect them or because they will in some way in a democratic society have opportunities to take a part in influencing the outcome. (Crick, 1998, p57)

Finally, in these examples there is a clear idea of a concept to be developed: the teachers concerned are initiating the teaching because they wish the learners to form some kind of abstract, transferable idea at the end of the process. This is an interpretation of citizenship which goes much further that the conception of learning to vote for politicians who will make decisions, and volunteering to help others in the community. Active citizens make efforts to understand what is going on, and to act on their analyses.

Behind many of the earlier attempts to engage children in the controversial was the idea of a network of broad social concepts, that it was argued, could be used to organise analysis, comparison and contrast. Conceptual frameworks for learning were increasingly popular in the 1970s: Bruner's work in the *MACOS* project (Bruner, 1966a) and Senesh's programme *Our Working World* (Senesh, 1968) illustrated how social, political and economic concepts could be developed in school students. They built up concepts through repeated exposure to case studies, and through strategies which encourage the learner to note, discuss and mark similarities, and thus understand the abstraction encompassed in the concept. The innovation was in the recognition that the abstraction, the concept, was best not taught directly, as a definition. However, to be useful, abstract concepts need some shared contextual meanings, and to develop these, we need to trade the words about, to use them with references to our experiences, so that we use them in a way that others understand. This is why classroom discussion must take place, so that meanings can be jointly constructed, not rote-learned in isolation (Bruner and Haste, 1987)

One problem that this approach can lead to is to over-emphasise the issues, or the experiential element of the learning. It is possible to develop an approach through a whole series of important social and political issues, which will engage the children, focus on experiences, arouse concern – but which are not harnessed to any underlying conceptual structures or frameworks. A teacher can develop lively classroom topics on environmental issues, but without an attempt to encourage reflection on the principles of political behaviour that lie behind them, a valuable educational experience is lost. Children need to construct a view of adult behaviour that enables them to see competing interests, power structures, systems of law construction and of justice and authority systems that underpin how these issues are dealt with, and why they are issues. This contrasts starkly with a strong primary ideology towards a consensual view – that the world should be presented to young children in a mawkish and maudlin way. Teachers and trainee teachers tend to want to present complex social issues in terms of simple solutions, with clearly defined 'good' and 'bad' perspectives. Thus Steiner (1992, 1996), evaluating how teachers approach world studies, concluded that

> Most teachers concentrate on the self-esteem building, interpersonal and cooperative element of the world studies approach. They also engage in work that questions stereotypes such as racism or sexism. The environment, local or 'rain forest', is a common theme. Global issues, such as those to do with the injustice inherent in the current systems of the global economy, or highlighting the cultural achievements and self-sufficiency of Southern societies ... receive far less attention. (Steiner, 1992, p9)

A more recent study by Robbins *et al* (2003) came to similar conclusions: trainee teachers seem to lack the confidence or expertise needed to translate their positive attitude toward education for global citizenship into classroom practice. A more radical view of the curriculum may be necessary to effect the necessary changes in attitude.

It is also tempting to take short cuts, or to mistake the outcome for the process. Given a conceptual map, or a grouping of key concepts (as given, for example by Crick, 1974), it is possible to offer children ready-made, hand-me-down definitions or summaries, that become the 'correct' answer. For example, guidelines for primary teachers in social studies produced in 1980 offered definitions such as

> *Power* is the ability to make others do as you want them to. *Authority* is based on the respect and obedience given to someone because of some official post that they hold and because they are agreed to have some personal ability and excellence in the task. ... All groups and societies exert *social control* on the behaviour of their members by making and defending rules and laws, and by expecting people to conform to certain conventions. (ILEA, 1980, p7-8)

Given such definitions, it is all too easy to teach these summaries directly to children, rather than helping children to construct their meaning through repeated exposure to examples and discussion about these. This is one of the traditions of the pedagogue in popular culture and experience: the teacher knows, and tells the learner what is to be known. This leads to a model of transmitting accepted knowledge: politics is a structured activity with defined institutions, procedures and conventions. When one has the facts, the knowledge, then one can begin to understand political activity. This is the kind of political education that politicians (*pace* chapter four) would have us promote: explanations of the wonders of the existing system that confirm the legitimacy of politicians to the young, and the justice and the equity that they promote. This reinforces the uncontroversial and bland. The trouble is that the pupils know better: they are aware that despite its rhetoric, the system isn't handling a whole range of social, political and economic issues that concern them – racism, poverty, the environment, housing, pollution, corruption. If one wants to engage children in a learning process about politics, one has to start with the issues that concern them. Children do have such concerns, as evidenced, for example, in the findings of Hilary Claire (2001), which articulate the clear and often strong views children hold about the world around them – about family and the politics of family life, about gender and sex, identity and racism, economic and social inequality.

Jerome Bruner argued in *Towards a Theory of Instruction* that

> human beings have three ways of knowing-through action, through imagery, and through the medium of symbols. Each is a system with powers and shortcomings, but the special glory of man's mind is that he has three approaches to grasping things, and these are often translatable into each other in a fashion that permits not only deeper understanding but the ferreting out of contradiction and nonsense. (Bruner, 1966b)

Bruner elaborated three modes of knowing:

- Enactive, where a person learns about the world through actions on objects

- Iconic, where learning occurs through using models and pictures

- Symbolic, which describes the capacity to think in abstract terms

Bruner argued that we should teach what he calls the structure of subjects. He advocated the introduction of the real process of a particular discipline to students. So, in learning history, students might become involved in genuine historical enquiry. This might entail examining a building, then using the information acquired to trace records of various kinds in order to answer the questions generated about the origins, purposes, and history of that structure:

> To instruct someone... is not a matter of getting him to commit results to mind. Rather, it is to teach him to participate in the process that makes possible the establishment of knowledge. We teach a subject not to produce little living libraries on that subject, but rather to get a student to think mathematically for himself, to consider matters as an historian does, to take part in the process of knowledge-getting. Knowing is a process not a product. (Bruner, 1966a, p72)

Bruner's underlying principle for teaching and learning is that a combination of concrete, pictorial and symbolic activities will lead to more effective learning. The progression is to start with a concrete experience then move to pictures and finally use symbolic representation. Active learning will be explored in more detail in chapter eight.

Studies of socio-political learning show that in many societies young children rapidly pick up iconic forms of the nation state and the community – for example American six year-olds recognise the flag, the presidency, the White House and Congress (see, for example, Hess and Torney, 1967; Easton and Dennis, 1969; Connell,1971; Coles, 1986); and then, later in their schooling, are introduced to the symbolic or conceptual representation, through civics lessons that describe the structures and processes, the lists of rights and duties. However, it is rarer for students to critically engage in enactive forms of citizenship. Active citizenship is not simply about voluntary activity and service learning: this can simply be ameliorative – while socially useful, it does not in itself provide learning about analysing social conditions or understanding the reasons for social inequality. Active citizenship requires the ability to engage in action for social change, the establishment of active solidarity, and the extension of rights: of necessity, it is engaging in debate, discussion and controversy, and using skills of engaging with and arguing with alternative viewpoints.

Such an approach suggests that we need to consider how learning and education happen in cooperative contexts. Engaging in social action, and in social discourse that advances viewpoints and ideas, requires collaborative approaches to learning. Much educational practice makes assumptions about the naturalness of competition, but there is evidence and arguments that societies have a far greater need for and reliance on collaboration. This is particularly interesting in the European Union context, because the Union is premised on balancing a tension between competition and cooperation: the economic aspects of the Union centre on the prosperity and security that should follow the economic competition that will be stimulated by free markets in trade, capital and labour. However, the inequalities that may be caused by this are simultaneously ameliorated through the social aspects of the union, that champion governmental action to control and manage commercial competition, to provide social care and economic safety nets for the population. The following chapter will begin with a brief examination of these tensions in contemporary European society, building on the markers for European identities that were highlighted at the end of chapter four, and will then explore the sociological evidence for cooperative behaviour.

Civic education has a strong tradition of transmitting symbolic and iconic aspects of citizenship. Bruner's third way of knowing, enactive learning, is less evident. Active learning requires engagement. How we can translate this abstract conceptual knowledge into enactive forms will develop out of our understanding of cooperative behaviour.

6

Cooperation and Competition: a social and a European tension

In chapter three it was suggested that European identity in the past had been characterised by the predominance of xenophobia and nationalism, of othering and exclusiveness, and of imperial domination. War appeared to dominate European history, particularly in the first half of the twentieth century. This has largely changed. Sheehan (2008) has recently observed from a trans-Atlantic perspective that in the late 20th and early 21st centuries

> most of Europe, the overwhelming majority of people came to view violence, both domestic and international, as something to be feared and avoided, not applauded or excused. . . . It seemed as if the experiences of the twentieth century had finally taught Europeans that such turmoil was an aberration, a pathological assault on normal society, something to be combated and overcome, like crime. (Sheehan, 2008, p181)

There has been an almost conscious turning against this old Europe. Solana's rejection of the Westphalian system, and its neglect of human rights (1998), and Fischer's rejection of nation-states' sovereign rights (2000) are also seen in Soysal's analysis of European school history text books over the past two decades: she identifies the presentation of Europe as future-orientated, rather than focused on the past; a Europe that no longer contrasts itself with the other (2002, 2006). She argues that current school texts acknowledge that 'European' characteristics of rights, society and welfare are not a monopoly of Europeans, and that there is little that is unique or original in the distinction of the European.

71

There are, however, some characteristics of contemporary Europe that are distinctive and, while not unique, sufficiently different from most other societies in the world. The European Union, in particular, is based on a creative tension between an open internal market, and the competitive environment that this creates, in capital, goods and labour, and a social model that seeks to deliberately mediate and protect citizens from the rigours that the market brings. The arbitration between competition and cooperation has been a fundamental driver in the Union's activities. This is not to argue that a proper balance has yet been struck, but that the need to find a pathway has been engaged with. Before analysing the social roles of competition and cooperation, it is useful to establish the defining characteristics of Europe's current and developing identity, expanding on the points that were briefly outlined at the end of chapter three.

European society is characterised by its social and cultural diversity, which is in many parts of Europe seen as something to be valued and supported. While it gives Europe great strength, it also presents challenges, and is a characteristic challenged by racists and xenophobes. European society is nevertheless broadly united in a fundamental belief in equality, linked to a desire to challenge and counter inequalities, to promote social cohesion, and to work for distributive justice. But its diversity also means, almost inevitably, that there are also inequalities and disadvantaged groups – socially, economically and culturally – and there are various strategies being attempted to address these inequalities, whilst also striving to preserve the diversity. Europeans have different histories, boundaries, disputes and languages, and they want to keep this cultural variety alive.

European social values are not in themselves unique. Some are shared by some other nations and regions of the world. But they are nevertheless a particular combination, articulated in a distinctive way. They also have a degree of fragility, and need to be defended and extended, and they are not always put into practice effectively. There are five particular areas in which European society has a distinct and positive identity, though within each there are practices that need to be improved, challenged and developed, and each of these positive characteristics contains some flaws.

Human rights

Contemporary Europe is founded on essential and legally enshrined human rights. Though these are well-developed, they will continue to need to be extended to address the needs of new and newly identified minorities. The fact that individuals and groups in Europe have access to a supranational and enforceable system of human rights, that has authority over national governments, is an important and unique feature of European society. These European human rights can be a positive factor in the global context, and there are examples of other countries amending their own human rights practices in order to work with Europe. But caution is needed so as not to impose or force systems based on the European perception of human rights and democracy on other states.

Europe has had a particular role in addressing global poverty and international development. Of course, much global inequality has arisen as a result of past European activities in colonialism and global exploitation, but Europe does now provide disproportionately more international aid than other developed countries, although the continent still falls considerably short of the UN target of 0.7% of Gross National Product. Of all the people in the world who live in countries where capital punishment is illegal, two thirds live in Europe. Europe generally also imprisons a much smaller proportion of its population – about a fifth of the level in the United States and Russia. These are important markers for the strength of European society's cooperative values.

Although these human rights are systemised and well developed, practice is varied, and there is also a perception of a fortress Europe; international action is not always accepted; sometimes there is a lack of trust; solidarity may be confined to certain groups or regions; and Europe's attitude towards the Third World is ambivalent. There is a rather two-faced attitude towards human rights beyond Europe, sometimes ignoring human rights when there are economic self-interests. Although corruption levels are relatively low in Europe, there remains much room for improvement.

Social Welfare

The second area that distinguishes European society is its provision of social welfare. Europe shares a broadly common idea of social welfare and of the role of the state in this. But welfare is unequally distributed, and varies between different social groups. Social welfare remains primarily embedded at the national level and is sometimes problematic at the European level. It has developed since 1945 in a different way in each country: although national welfare systems are diverse, and give different roles to the family, the state, insurance and private companies, they all share a conviction that the disadvantaged are not to be blamed as being responsible for their own misfortune, and that society collectively and cooperatively has the responsibility to care for disadvantaged groups, to support and to empower them to participate and to minimise inequalities. Social resources are not distributed fairly and there is competition between individuals, so that there is a continuing need to protect, modify and extend our social welfare systems. Europe has a distinctive and positive model of welfare, affordable through relatively high taxation policies.

Education

Education in European is broadly based on principles of free and universal access, and an open attitude towards knowledge. Education helps individuals to achieve both vertical and horizontal mobility in the emerging European context, and efforts to harmonise educational provision and qualifications are trying to support this. However, educational systems are never value-free, and are not therefore always well-adapted for diverse social groups. Aspects of Europe's diversity mean that some social groups continue to have unequal access to education, or to success in education, and thus to the advantages that education can bring. Access is not well-distributed, and some groups have limited ability to participate fully while other groups tend to competitively preserve and protect their particular positions and advantages. Despite these caveats, the processes of ensuring a European-wide framework for educational provision are leading to substantially greater levels of debate about the goals, purposes and means of education that are found in most other parts of the world.

Physical and social mobility

This fourth important characteristic image of Europe arises from the increasing level of mobility, for study, employment and for leisure. Tourism and mobility for professional reasons lead to a rise of social citizenship; student mobility breaks down barriers, decreases scepticism and broadens the individual's views about the cultural values of others. It encourages networking and insights into the lives of others elsewhere and in other professional circumstances. Mobility, and the social contacts that follow from living in a different country, can add significantly to the individual's understanding of European society and diversity. But labour mobility may be limited to particular groups, and may also lead to resentment and friction. There are barriers to the mobility of disabled people and certain economic, social and ethnic groups. There are risks of an increasing social gap and tensions between states and regions in the EU. Not everyone is welcome in other parts of Europe; xenophobia is much more evident among non-mobile groups. Mobility in Europe has yet to be extended from a relatively elite group to all, and inequalities in access to mobility need to be addressed.

Languages and communication

The fifth characteristic of European society is our attitude towards language and communication. Languages are a tool for social communication, and this is important to support mutual understanding, and European Union's 'one plus two' language policy (for everyone to add to their first language two more languages) attempts to preserve linguistic diversity and to improve understanding and appreciation of diversity. The ability to communicate in more than one language is relevant for the job market, is linked to mobility, but also to social elites: knowledge of languages helps horizontal and vertical mobility. Inequalities arise when groups and individuals have differential access to and competences in some languages. Ability in English in particular may privilege particular elites. Europe is also reluctant to value the non-European languages spoken by many minorities: valuing them might lead to greater respect for peoples with such competences.

A major characteristic of European society is how its members are able to learn from each other: diversity becomes a very positive aspect of this. Europe has learned from its history, and its members are learning to trust each other, to be reflective, and to use best practice. The Union is based on both establishing a common civic tradition and on developing a shared regulatory market economy. The former implies the development of a high degree of cooperation and trust between individuals and groups; the latter that individuals and groups engage in competition to provide goods and services. How do these two characteristics of cooperation and competition interact? Evaluating this will help identify the qualities needed to support the practices of citizenship. This chapter will now explore some of the sociological issues around cooperation and competition in contemporary and historically recent societies, and relate these to conceptions of citizenship and enterprise.

Adam Smith is often upheld as an early key exponent of competitive enterprise. Yet, as the following quotation from *The Wealth of Nations* shows, even in the apparently competitive setting of the free market, individuals and groups will seek to cooperate, and not always to compete.

> People of the same trade seldom meet together, even for merriment and diversion, but the conversation ends in a conspiracy against the public, or in some contrivance to raise prices. (Smith, 1776, p128)

We need to examine competitive behaviours by and between groups, as well as cooperation between individuals and groups. Competition and cooperation may be taking place simultaneously in the same activity: for example, in many team games there is necessarily intra-team game cooperation to support in inter-team competition: the two forms of behaviour need not be seen as polar opposites, or alternative ways of conducting relationships. This is true also in educational settings (Ross, Fülöp and Kuščer, 2006). The PISA study (Programme for International Student Assessment) (*Knowledge and*

Skills for Life, Organisation for Economic Cooperation and Development (OECD), 2001) created comparative international indices for cooperative and competitive learning, based on what students reported in a survey. The cooperative indices were based on questions about whether students liked working with others and helping others, while the competitive index was based on responses to questions about whether students liked to do better than others (being the best, learning better when trying to be better than others) (OECD, 2001, p114). Of the 24 countries in this study Hungary scored third lowest on cooperative learning and eighth highest on competitive learning. This was unusual: Haahr *et al* (2005) note that:

> paradoxically, many countries where students have relatively high scores on the index of cooperative learning are also the countries where students have correspondingly high scores on the index of competitive learning, and *vice versa*. (p128)

For example, in an analysis of the survey of reading (Kirsch *et al*, 2000), United Kingdom students scored particularly highly in their preference for cooperative learning (third out of 22 states), and in competitive learning they also scored highly (seventh out of 22) (Haahr *et al*, 2005).The OECD report suggested that probably 'active learners use both strategies on different occasions, rather than limiting themselves to a single strategy that may not be the best in a particular situation' (OECD, 2001, p115).

The two activities of competition and cooperation are often seen as being attached to particular moral values. Societies and economies have been predicated and constructed on ideologies that are based around one or the other. Systems based on each have claimed that their preferred characteristic offers a particularly virtuous way of organising society, and at the same time have demonised the other's approach. The conditions for competitive economic behaviour set out in traditional market economics are based on a series of assumptions. These include the concept of an economically rational individual, who always behaves to maximise their own interest and good, and the idea that the market operates in conditions in which individuals – whether producers or consumers – have perfect and accurate knowledge. Much traditional economics is based on a psychological construct of the individual: the aggregated behaviour of these economic individuals is held to govern the way in which markets operate (through what Adam Smith called 'the invisible hand' of the market). There is an emerging body of literature that now challenges many of these assumptions. Individuals and groups do not always act in a wholly self-interested or competitive way, and markets are rarely perfect. Self-interest is a particularly important concept to examine in relation to competitive and cooperative behaviours.

Adam Smith is credited with being the first to explain the operation of the market. It is often suggested that he advocated individuals should operate in a wholly self-interested manner, developing their own wealth at the expense of others. However, he pointed out that 'no society can flourish (where) the far greater part of its members are poor and miserable', and was highly critical of the operation of the free market as he saw it affecting the society around him. He thought a society and economy in which 'a mother who has borne twenty children' saw most die in infancy was misgoverned. He argued for publicly funded mass education, and for a road system that was free for users, unlike the then common toll-road system, and the public provision of social enterprises such as lighthouses – acknowledging that none of these could be provided by relying on 'the market'. From this first analysis of the operation of the market, it was acknowledged that a society that operated only from self-interest would be flawed, and that the market needed to be carefully regulated and reined in by government in order to protect workers, both individually and as group.

> Whenever the legislature attempts to regulate the differences between masters and their workmen, its counsellors are always the masters. When the regulation, therefore, is in favour of the work-men, it is always just and equitable; but it is sometimes otherwise when in favour of the masters. (Smith, 1776, Book 1, Chapter 10).

As the earlier quotation from Smith suggests, he displayed a healthy cynicism about the motivations of those who took advantage of the market:

> It is not from the benevolence of the butcher, the brewer, or the baker that we expect our dinner, but from their regard to their own interest. We address ourselves not to their self-love, and never talk to them of our own necessities but of their advantages. (Smith, 1776, p129)

So Smith was not suggesting that people, simply by acting solely in their own self-interest, would benefit the community around them: it would be necessary to have a conscious regard for community service. In other words, self-interest did not necessarily equate with general interest. He did not argue that people *should* act in their own self interest, but described his observations of economic behaviour – that people *do* act in their own interest. It will be argued below that even this is not necessarily so, and that individuals often behave in ways other than self-interest. Smith did not claim that *all* self-interest had a beneficial effect on the community, or that it was always good; he only held that self-interest was not necessarily bad.

Historical studies of the growth of mercantilism and of complex economic production, trade and marketing suggest that much of the development was conditional upon the growth of trust and cooperation between individuals and between groups of traders. Smith pointed out that 'when the greater part of people are merchants they always bring probity and punctuality into fashion'. The growth of the Hanseatic League – trading ports in different countries in the North Sea and Baltic, that operated a code of practice relating that supported acceptances of bonds and credit, rather than coin and gold – is an early example.

Richard Tilly's (1983) study of 18th century business shows the development of an understanding by those engaged in commerce that, if they were able to trust each other and to cooperate in behaving, these particular norms allowed them to prosper, and that the perception that honesty was profitable would spread. Tilly argues that the growth of the Quaker merchants in the early eighteenth century was largely dependent on the fact that they could rely on each other to be honest, to meet debts, to honour promises, and to reliably supply quality goods and services between each other: with this degree of certainty behind them, they could invest their energies into production and trade, rather than ensuring that the terms of trade were enforced. This was personal trust, based on a close social/ religious network (literally, 'The Society of Friends'). Nearly all modern commercial relationships depend on trust and cooperation in everyday transactions. Such behaviour allows the accumulation of long term capital. Violating this trust in order to make short term gains may produce greater immediate riches, but means that long term relationships cannot be established, and ultimately less wealth will be accumulated.

Examples of the development of capitalist proponents of trust in 19th century American commerce include the showman P T Barnum, who pioneered customer services, Wannamaker, who introduced the novel idea of standardising fixed prices in trade rather than spending time and effort in negotiating prices afresh for each transaction, and the steel magnate Morgan, who built many businesses on the basis of trust in his personal reputation. If Morgan was a director of a company, investors trusted his integrity that the company was sound, and invested. Tilly describes how businessmen thus started to see 'individual transactions as links in a larger chain of profitable business ventures', and not as 'one-time opportunities to be exploited to the utmost'. This trust had now become impersonal, and was no longer based on personal connections, as had been the case with the Quakers.

Contemporary economic organisations, and many modern commercial developments, demonstrate cooperative as well as competitive behaviour. One notable recent example of this is the development of open source software. The Norwegian Linus Torvalds developed the Linus system for computer operating systems in 1991: this allows anyone to use the software, freely and without charge, solely on the condition that they acknowledge the sources and make any improvements they add equally open to all. Improvements are haphazard and effectively decentralised, and the lack of formal organisation allows diversity and product improvement, all of which is based on cooperation between programmers (Kowabura, 2000; Torvalds, 2001).

Commenting on this, Kelty (2001) points to similar principles of non-propietorial ownership underpinning modern science:

> open source is not 'like' science, it is *part* of science. If we ask where free software flourished in the period from 1984 to the present, then the answer is: as part of the institutions of science. ... When open source and free software advocates compare free software to science, and the scientific method, they usually make the claim, often explicitly, that through some unspecified mechanism this open, collaborative, non-proprietary community of software development actually results in *better* software, whether indirectly through debugging or directly through openness and deliberative design. Indeed, even across the lines drawn between them, the Open Source organization and the Free Software Foundation agree on this: guaranteed openness creates better, more stable, less buggy software – software that does not suck. (Kelty, 2001, p1-2)

Collaboration in science and academia is now the norm: for example, the paper in 1994 that announced the discovery of the quark sub-atomic particle credited 450 physicists. This 'division of cognitive labour' allows the incorporation of many different kinds of knowledge in an active way, and guarantees a diversity of perspectives. Writing on the economics of scientific production, Stephan claims that collaboration makes each individual more productive: 'scientists who collaborate with each other are more productive, often producing 'better' science, than individual investigators'(1996, p1201). Studies of scientific collaboration point out that the more frequently a scientist works with others, the more productive and better known he or she is likely to be (Solla Price and Beaver, 1966): studying scientific publications, they found that 'the most prolific man [*sic*] is also by far the most collaborating, and three of the next four most prolific are also among the next most frequently collaborating' (Solla Price and Beaver, 1966, p1014; see also Wenger, 2002). This collaboration is not through self-interest, or for aggrandisement of esteem or reputation: a study by Zuckerman (1967) which compared 41 Nobel laureates to scientists in the same field, with similar reputations, found that the laureates collaborated far more often than non-laureates, pre and post-award: post-award they would have nothing to gain from collaborating – though those with whom they collaborated might – but nevertheless still collaborated:

> Science in fact depends on collective activity, and information is not hoarded but made freely available. Popper points out in *The Logic of Scientific Discovery* (1959) that this is the very basis of inductive scientific method and advance, publication making it possible to refute hypotheses and findings, and becoming the basis others can use to construct new hypotheses. 'The assumption is that society as a whole will end up knowing more if information is diffused as widely as possible, rather than being limited to a few people. (Surowiecki, 2003, p164).

Scientists and other academics do compete for recognition and attention, but the attention that they seek can only be given by those against whom they compete. Thus scientific enterprises – like many other productive and service enterprises – are both competitive and cooperative. The desire to achieve recognition requires that they frequently publish new hypotheses and syntheses. This can be traced back to the mid 17th century, even earlier than mercantilist cooperation, when the English Royal Society published the first issue of *Philosophical Transactions* in 1665. The first secretary of the society, and editor of the *Transactions,* Henry Oldenburg, argued that secrecy was not compatible with scientific progress: the scientist should relinquish their sole ownership of the ideas that they had developed in exchange for public recognition and acknowledgement as the creator or discoverer. The peculiar characteristic of knowledge is that it does not get used up or consumed, and so can be spread widely and still retain its value (Jardine, 1999). The sharing of new knowledge heralded the period of the scientific revolution,

> in which 'open' science emerged, when knowledge about the natural world became increasingly non-proprietorial and scientific advances and discoveries were freely shared with the public at large. Thus scientific knowledge became a public good, freely communicated, rather that confined to a secretive few as had been the custom in medieval Europe. (Mokyr, 2002, p291)

The sociologist Robert Merton pointed out that 'in science, one's private property is established by giving its substance away' (1988, p620), and this notion of transactions that are based on a gift economy, rather than an exchange economy, is not confined to science (Hagstrom, 1982; see also Richard Titmuss (1971) on the gift economy in areas such as blood donation). These arguments have particular relevance to collaboration and competition in contemporary Europe: the knowledge based economy is a major target that the European Union aspires to create (European Union 1997), an intention reiterated at the Lisbon European Council meeting (European Union, 2000b).

Turning from group cooperation to individual pro-social behaviour, various recent studies in economic psychology have examined individual decision-making processes, and have challenged the conception of the economically rational individual, who always operates in terms of his or her self-interest. This is not the same as the phenomena of individuals operating independently to solve coordination problems (the 'El Farol problem', Arthur, 1994; Bell and Sethares, 2001). The Ultimatum Game has been used in a wide variety of societies, and presents a serious challenge to pure self-interest theory. In this game, two individuals who do not know each other are brought together for a one-off encounter. They are told that one of them will be asked to divide a single sum of money – typically an average day's wage – into two amounts, in any proportion that they chose. The other person may then decide to accept the sum offered – in which case, both participants take their allotted share – or to reject the offer, in which case neither gets anything. Whatever the decision or the outcome, the game is over and not repeated, so there is no possible calculated trade-off as to what might happen in a second 'round' of the game. Traditional economic realism would suggest that the participant making the division should split the sum in such a way that they maximise their income, and minimise the fraction offered. Equally, self-interest should mean that a participant offered a miniscule fraction, say five per cent, would argue that this is better than nothing, and accept it. In fact, participants over a very wide range of societies show that people's behaviour is not 'rational'. Most prefer a much fairer division, the person making the offer generally offering between 40 and 50 per cent – and the person accepting generally refusing to take less than 30 per cent. Most people prefer a fairer split, rather than one taking most (Smith, 2003; Roth and Prasniker, 1991).

These studies, repeated widely around the world, have recently been attempted in non-advanced societies of hunter-gathers, pastoralists and nomads (Henrich *et al*, in press). Similar pro-social behaviour was observed, though not as great as in the 'advanced' societies considered in most of the earlier studies. But the degree of pro-social behaviour was greater in situations where there was more advanced social and economic interdependence in the culture. This correlation suggests that cooperative and pro-social behaviour develops with social and economic interaction, in just the same way that the Quaker industrialists discovered that trust in trading and dealing was easier and more worthwhile that relying on short-term gains based on lack of trust.

Pro-sociality becomes stronger because it works. Bowles and Gintis (2003) argue that many people exhibit a characteristic they describe as strong reciprocity, which is a willingness to reward good behaviour and to punish bad behaviour, even when doing so brings no material benefit to the individual. Such pro-social behaviour occurs when people go beyond the narrow definitions of self-interest and do things that are in the common good. People who are strong reciprocators behave in his way because they react against what they see as violations of their personal sense of what is just. They do so, not necessarily for reasons of simple altruism or humanitarianism, but because of a sense of equity, though the outcome would be the same if their behaviour was purely altruistic. The effect is the same: offers made are generally equitable, inequitable behaviour is punished, even at the expense of self-interest (Bowles and Gintis, 2003; Hammerstein, 2003; Fehr and Gachter, 2000a).

These proclivities have not been substantially explored with school students as yet. The work of Henrich *et al*, referred to above, suggests that at least part of such behaviour is contingent upon the socio-economic complexity and must therefore be socially learned behaviour. It is therefore of considerable interest to know not just how such learning takes place, but what, if any teaching activities might encourage such learning. Murnigham *et al* (1998) conducted a series of hypothetical ultimatum games with k grade, 3rd and 6th grade children in Illinois: in these experiments the participants were asked to *imagine* that another child had made a division, and asked to respond. Moreover, there were no actual rewards – it was judged unethical to give the respondents any sweets or money as a result of the decision. Nevertheless, they found that younger children would 'accept' less equal offers than older children. Harbaugh *et al* (2002) conducted a series of bargaining games, including the ultimatum game, with children between 7 and 18 in fairly isolated communities in Oregon. Unfortunately, the experimenters violated some of the principles of the ultimatum game: in particular the children were told that they would play more than once, and may thus have been induced to act strategically. They found that even at the age of 7 bargaining strategies had been developed, and that generally children made and accepted smaller amounts than adults, and they suggested that there are changes in samples from the same culture over different ages. They also noted a series of gender differences. Mittone (2003) worked with 9 and 12 year-olds in Trento, Italy, using a different game of pattern-making to investigate 'ethically altruistic behaviour': he concluded that at both ages there is a high propensity to cooperate – higher than that of adults. Sutter (2005) worked with a small sample of Austrian children aged between 7 and 10 using the ultimatum game: he was primarily interested in the relationship between rejection rates and the availability of alternative offers. He found that children rejected unequal offers more than students, suggesting that for the children fairer outcomes were more important than perceptions of fair intentions.

These studies of group and individual cooperative behaviour and competitive behaviour suggest that there is a far more complex relationship between them than might at first be supposed, and that neither offers a complete account that will explain behaviour in a complex society. Knack and Keefer (2001) demonstrate that the

advantages of commonly accepted and agreed patterns of cooperation are that individuals in higher trust societies spend less to protect
themselves from being exploited in economic transactions. Written
contracts are less likely to be needed, and they do not have to specify
every possible contingency. More recently, Benabou and Tirole
(2005) have attempted to bring these studies together, developing a
theory of pro-social behaviour that combines heterogeneity in
individual altruism and greed with concerns for social reputation or
self-respect. They argue that rewards or punishments raise questions
about the motivation of pro-social deeds, and that extrinsic incentives can crowd out pro-social behaviour.

Neither do commercial firms necessarily behave in a competitive
manner. They certainly do not do so internally. Suroweicki points out
that 'the fundamental paradox of any corporation is that even though
it competes in the market place, it used non-market instruments –
plans, commands, controls – to accomplish its goals' (2004, p195).
Robertson described corporations as 'islands of conscious power in
this ocean of unconscious cooperation, like lumps of butter
coagulating in a pail of buttermilk' (cited in Coase, 1988). Different
parts of a firm cooperate, and are created in order to cooperate with
the other parts of the firm, rather than outsourcing supply and
engaging in the uncertain and probably expensive transaction costs
involved in setting up and monitoring deals and contacts, including
search and information costs, bargaining and decision costs and
policing and enforcement costs. Mechanisms within the firm designed to encourage internal competition are generally ineffective,
and lead to workers and managers conspiring against the firm. Roy's
classic shop floor study (1952) of lathe operators in a machine shop
operating a piece rate incentive scheme showed how operatives
realised that if they work too hard or fast, then the incentive schemes
that operated would curtail their incentives. Instead of working out
how to be most productive, they spent considerable time in working
out how to manipulate the rate per piece. The same principle is seen
operating at executive and management levels in the firm. Targets
are set in 'management by objectives' schemes: executives typically
manipulate the system to ensure that they are set low targets, and

then, when targets have been set, manipulate the system to show that they have achieved the maximum gain (Jensen, 2001a, 2001b).

Government – and thus citizens in their relationship with government – have a close and important role to play in the promotion of both competitive enterprise and in cooperative behaviour. We noted above that Adam Smith insisted on the role of government in protecting and safeguarding the poor and exploited against the excesses of capitalist greed. Governments act to regulate trade, often to ensure that competition is equitable. Legislation proscribes monopolistic behaviour that acts against the individual consumer, and price fixing cartels. Legislation protects consumers by ensuring that goods are of quality, that they are not harmful, that they are clearly labelled to identify quantities and ingredients. Without this promotion of free competition – by insisting on consumers being given sufficient knowledge and information to make a reasonably informed choice – the nature of the market might conspire to make competition impossible. At the same time, governments actively promote cooperation; they need to encourage – and at time require – citizens to act in the public interest, rather than in terms of self-interest.

In this they are frequently successful. The payment of taxes is a classic example of a cooperation problem. Much government expenditure is on what are called non-excludable goods and services – things that everyone benefits from, and from which it is not easy to exclude people from benefiting. Adam Smith's classic example was the lighthouse, that protected all seafarers from shipwreck, whether they contributed to the cost of erecting and maintaining the lighthouse or not. Today, all benefit from national expenditure on defence, policing, transport infrastructure, public education and public health, whether or not an individual pays tax or not. Self-interest would suggest that the rational course of action would be to cheat, and to avoid paying taxes. There is a low likelihood of being caught. But most people cooperate and pay taxes. It may be individually costly, but it is collectively beneficial, and only works if nearly everyone takes part. Margaret Levi argues that most taxpayers are 'contingent consenters'

– they consent if everyone else is doing so (1999). Various experimental games in economic psychology suggest that sufficient of the population in most advanced societies understand and accept the need to contribute (Fehr and Gachter, 2000b). Less than 15 per cent are selfish (or 'rational', in the classic economic sense) – and try to free-ride. Altruists are a similar sized minority, who will continue to contribute to public pot, even when others are clearly free-riding. Most people are conditional consenters, and will contribute to taxes as long as they feel and perceive that most other people are doing so. But if their perception is that others are free-riding, then their contributions will begin to decline.

Where can we locate citizenship in this mix of competitive and co-operative behaviour? Do modern societies seek civic democratic involvement because it gives a sense of involvement and control over lives and this contributes to stability, or because individuals have the right to rule themselves, or as a way of making intelligent decisions and uncovering the truth? Again, we can see democratic participation as evidence of acting against self-interest, and behaving in a co-operative, pro-social manner. For example, it is not rational to take part in elections: the act of an individual in voting is extremely unlikely to have a direct effect of the result. Yet large numbers of people vote, because others vote, and the collective result does in some way represent a collective judgement. How do people vote? A study in the late 1970s in the USA suggested that people do not select for whom they will vote on the basis of their own personal economic well-being, but on how they perceive the general economy to be behaving (Kinder and Kiewiet, 1979, 1981). There was a substantial correlation between how voters saw the economy performing as a whole and how they vote, and virtually no correlation with their own personal economic position. Sears and Funk (1990) found that voters' ideological predilections were a much better predictor of their attitudes on issues than self-interest: they give examples from the USA of conservatives who did not have health insurance opposing national health insurance schemes, and liberals with private health insurance who nevertheless favour the introduction of a national health insurance scheme.

Given this complexity, and the suggestion by Henrich *et al* (in press) that pro-social and cooperative behaviour may be socially learned and contingent on the socio-economic complexity of a society, the role of educators and schools in the process of developing coopera-tive – and perhaps competitive – behaviour is clearly of great interest. How do young people construct themselves and their identi-ties as cooperators and competitors? In developing their civic be-haviour, they operate in social conditions of both cooperation and competition: they will have an understanding of the differences and similarities in the ways in which their neighbours and fellow-citizens construct their own identities. An identity is competitive when it seeks to distinguish itself from others, and becomes cooperative when it seeks to align itself as a member of a group. The next chapter explores how different identities can be expressed by the same individual in different contexts, and how various identities relate to a sense of citizenship, or belonging – and to a sense of European-ness.

7

Singular and Multiple Identities

Identity is used in various ways in different disciplines in the social sciences. How individuals understand themselves as a distinct and detached being has different meanings and is analysed in different ways in psychology and in sociology: here I am adopting sociological and some social psychological perspectives. This discussion will thus not be particularly concerned with ideas of self-image, or the capacity an individual might have to reflect and be aware of themselves as an individual. It will focus rather on how individuals construct or negotiate their identity in social settings, describing or projecting themselves as members of particular groups, communities or as having particular social roles. This conceptualisation of identity has particular significance for citizenship, as one of the categories around which an identity can be constructed. The previous chapter has examined the balance between the co-operation and trust between individuals and groups and the competition between individuals and groups to provide and acquire goods and services: we now move to examine the relationship between the individual and groups, which is key to social identity and how the individual behaves in social collectivities.

In the Social Identity Theory proposed by Tajfel and Turner (1979) individuals tend to categorise themselves as members of one or more in-groups, constructing part of their identity as being a member of each group. They argued that a corollary of this is that individuals also create and maintain boundaries with other groups. This identification with group membership maximises the individual's distinctiveness, because the group offers an identity with positive esteem.

Individuals use categories to label themselves and others, as a parent, an Italian, or a worker, for example, and the categories they attach to themselves tend to be ones that support their own self-esteem. This means that other categories or groups may be, in comparison, less well-regarded in their view; the combination of these factors creates an identity that is distinct from, and in some way 'better' than those whom they see as belonging to other categories. These processes are thus individual and collective: the creation of social categories is only meaningful when it is done with others and shared in some way, but it is nevertheless carried out by each individual. The ascription of shared values to a group or category will not be universally held, of course: individuals who identify themselves as 'women', for example, may hold an approximately shared view of how their group differs from and in some ways may be more virtuous than the group they define as 'men'; while the 'men' may have a rather different view of their own group and its identity *vis-à-vis* 'women'. Not all females may use the category 'women' (of themselves, or of others), or in all contexts. This particular gendered dynamic will be itself different in different cultures and classes.

> Social identities ... are associated with normative rights, obligations and sanctions which, within specific collectivities, form roles. The use of standardized markers, especially to do with the bodily attributes of age and gender, is fundamental in all societies, notwithstanding large cross-cultural variations which can be noted. (Giddens, 1984, p281)

These categories or groupings take on a particular significance in the areas of national and ethnic identity.

There is a school of national identity that has its roots in the work of Herder, the 18th century German philosopher who proposed a romantic *volk* nationalism based exclusively on shared descent – a unity of 'blood and soil': in this interpretation, geography formed the natural economy of a people, and their customs and society would develop along the lines that their basic environment favoured (Herder, 1794). This idea of a national spirit or soul essentialises national identity into a unique and unchanging characteristic, based on fixed and objective criteria that include common biological descent. The alternative, social constructionist, standpoint is that identity – including national identity – is a matter of political choice, and is not a natural given. In the 1960s and 1970s assertions of ethnic identity were often seen as anachronisms, parallel to romantic nationalism: ethnic identity was frequently associated with so-called objective socio-biological measures. Critics saw such ethnicity as an outcome of political myth-making in the strategising of group advantage: Smith, for example, refers to ethnic groups as composed

> of people whose members share a common name and elements of culture, possess a myth of common origin and common historical memory, who associate themselves with a particular territory and possess a feeling of solidarity. (Smith, 1986, p15)

Ethnic identity was, from this perspective, simply a political strategy – a group struggling to assert primordial and distinctive values, yet also a group tied to 'race' and biological descent, an identity that was ascribed and immutable.

The social constructivist view of ethnicity and of national identity sees these as subjective terms, used to create a distinctive category. Barth (1969) suggested that ethnic groups created their own sense of being a group by actively creating symbolic boundaries: ethnic identity becomes what the group chooses and agrees it wants to be and have in common and how it wants to be different, rather than being based on fixed characteristics such as descent or language. The idea of boundary construction and maintenance helps explain how social organisation, order and group membership is maintained. The same set of ideas can be used to account for national identities, where the construction of bonds based on a presumption of shared group ideas, cultural artefacts and emotions is possible even where members do not know each other personally: Anderson (1983, 1991) describes national identities as *Imagined Communities*, a narrative that will be unravelled later in this chapter.

Culture can be seen as the way a social group promotes particular symbols that identify its uniqueness: the meanings of cultural symbols are not given, or fixed, but are created through social negotiation by members of the group. To give two current examples: the circumstances of the 1398 Battle of Kosovo in which the Serbs under Prince Lazar were defeated by the Turks have become some of the defining characteristics of contemporary Serbian identity and its territorial claim to Kosovo; and the definition of the *evenements de Mai* 1968 continue to be used to construct the shared identity of the *soixante-huitards*. These are symbolic statements and events that give meaning to the perceptions and behaviour of these two groups, and the meanings are not objective, but are created by the group as part of its way of viewing the rest of the world. This is not an individual activity, but is conducted, as Geertz observes, 'not in the head, but in that public world where people talk together, name things, make assertions, and to a degree understand each other' (1973, p213; also 1972).

There are tensions implicit in this. Firstly, the individual ascribes themselves membership of a group, and participates in some way in the definition of the group's boundaries. But these boundaries are subjective, and are also imaginary, in Anderson's definition – the individual can only imagine how other members of the group, the majority of whom they do not know and will never meet – are constructing *their* 'elastic' boundaries to the group. The idea that an ethnic identity can be generalised to all members of the group is difficult to sustain: it is even more difficult with reference to a national identity. Cohen (1994). points out that there is a continuous process of reconstructing ethnic identity within an ethnic group, by the individual members of the group. There are individual variations within all such groups, and the boundaries are determined by the concatenation of the constructs in the mind of each individual member, and the understanding of these boundaries will be not be understood exactly or equivalently (Cohen, 1998). Each member will define their group membership in their own particular way, using individual symbolic boundaries to construct the group. Many characteristics of a typical group identity may be held in common, but not all. Ethnic identity in particular is a construct dependent not just on external boundaries but also on the member's own definition of boundaries, which will not necessarily be held in common with others.

A second tension arises in the conscious ways in which group identities are now sometimes constructed. New social groups and minority nationalisms and ethnicities become perceived as constructs around which small social groups might gain or regain some level of control. Identity can be used as an ideological construct for political mobilisation through ethnicity and nationalism. Thus, for example, in a recent study of ethnic difference in secondary schools in England, France, Germany and the Netherlands, Mannitz concludes that the British positive action programmes for minorities 'trigger[s] off jealous competition among pupils based on ethnic group perceptions. The notion of a social mosaic creates segmentary boundary effects when pupils from ethnic minority groups measure and asses their individual chances of upward mobility' (2004a, p331).

To add to this complexity, the growing effects of globalisation are transforming social and cultural experiences, and thus changing concepts of identities. The movement of individuals, capital, consumer goods and technology – much of which has been accentuated by the European Union itself – has given rise to new configurations of identity, in an almost kaleidoscopic manner. Globalisation has been matched by localisation, and an increased regionalism. Many social scientists suggest that identity is no longer fixed and immutable, as many people increasingly define themselves in multiple ways. For example, Modood and Werbner (1997) describe identity as something that is fluid, shifting and multi-dimensional. Terms such as hybridised identities or hyphenated identities are increasingly used to capture the complexity of the cultural configurations and identities of contemporary societies. The idea of multiple identities, which will be explored at greater length later in this chapter, allows an individual to construct a range of identities around her or his personal experiences. Fass has explored such complex ranges of identities in ethnic and class terms amongst Turkish youth in Germany and the UK (2007, 2008). Sangrador (1996) and Moreno

(1997) show how individuals can express two or more territorial identities at the same time, demonstrating this through the way in which regional populations in Spain express both national identity and narrower collective regional identities, demonstrating the possible compatibility of several social, cultural and political attachments at the same time.

Gergen's work on the social construction of the individual (1994) goes further than this, and suggests that individuals may become strategic manipulators, who use the ascription of identity as a form of role-playing, simply acquiring badges that are thought to have particular strategic value. What he calls the 'pastiche personality' is an individual who uses social interaction to play out particular roles or identities.

Identity and citizenship have thus become concepts used with a wide variety of meanings. There have been many suggestions that individuals do not have singular identities, but a repertoire of different identities. The individual will use each of these, or a combination of them, contingently on where they are, whom they are with, and the particular social setting in which they find themselves (eg Hall, 1992, 1996, 1997). Stuart Hall attacked the idea that the individual was 'fully centred, unified ... endowed with capacities of reason, consciousness and action' (1992, p275), seeing identity instead as 'composed of not a single, but of several, sometimes contradictory or unresolved, identities' (*ibid*, p276-7). Amaryta Sen has attacked 'the fallacy of singular identity': he argues that 'forcing people into boxes of singular identity try[s] ... to understand human beings not as persons with diverse identities but predominantly as members of one particular social group or community' (Sen, 2006, p176), whereas we might wish to identify ourselves with a whole variety of possible identity descriptors, such as feminist, Asian, an Indian citizen, of Bengali origin, a British resident, a man, a non-believer, and a defender of gay and lesbian rights (Sen, 2006, p19). Sen reflects graphically on his experiences as a young boy in partition India in 1947, where he witnessed the killing of a Muslim family servant, identified solely on the singular identity of his religion.

Gundara cites a similar set of examples of young people's multiple identities, arguing that they contribute to meeting the challenge of how 'experimental democratic education can guarantee social integration in highly differentiated contexts' (Gundara, 2006, p25). Some of the identities that Sen and Gundara list can be grouped as related to place or geographic location, and in many cases these places nest one within another. Other of these identities could be classed as membership of or belonging to a group, such as British or working class, while others are descriptions of identity as set of relationships (such as friend, or parent).

The following example demonstrates the complexity of these multiplicities: The *Guardian* reported on Asmaa Abdol-Hamid, a Muslim Dane standing for election to the *Folketing*, the Danish Parliament (Traynor, 2007, p19):

> The 25-year-old social worker, student and town councillor describes herself as a feminist, a democrat, and a socialist. She has gay friends, opposes the death penalty, supports abortion rights, and could not care less what goes on in other people's bedrooms. In short, a tolerant Scandinavian and European.
>
> She is also a Palestinian and a devout Muslim who insists on wearing a headscarf, who refuses, on religious grounds, to shake hands with males, and who is bidding fair to be the first Muslim woman ever to enter the *Folketing*, the Danish parliament in Copenhagen.
>
> For the extreme right, the young activist is a political provocateur, an agent of Islamic fundamentalism bent on infiltrating the seat of Danish democracy. To many on the left, Ms Abdol-Hamid is also problematic, personifying through her dress the reactionary repression of women and an illiberal religious agenda that should have no place in her leftwing 'red-green' alliance of socialists and environmentalists.
>
> As a result of announcing her parliamentary candidacy earlier this month, the young Muslim and Danish citizen has been thrust to the centre of a debate tormenting Denmark and the rest of western Europe – on the place and values of Islam in modern Europe and the treatment of large Muslim minorities.

Ms Abdol-Hamid is unfazed. 'I see more Islam here in Denmark than in Iran or in other places in the Middle East,' she says. 'It's easier to be a Muslim in Denmark than in Saudi Arabia. I don't feel a stranger here. I'm interested in politics. I want to talk about this society, about political issues. But I'm not in politics because I'm a Muslim.'

.....

'Some Muslims don't think it's right for a female to act like this. They go to my father and tell him, get her married, get her married,' she laughs. 'Others think you can't be Muslim and Danish at the same time. Some of the Muslims and the extreme right are just the same'.

'And there are women in my party who say that anyone who wears the headscarf is oppressed. It's like they think I'm dumb. They're taking away my individuality. We need the right to choose. It's up to us whether or not we wear headscarves. They think I'm a woman from the Middle East. No. I'm a Danish Muslim.'

Identities thus become contingent. The identity or group of identities selected for presentation is a response to the group(s) that constitutes the audience, to the location of the encounter, and to the history and events that preceded it. To give a current example, a young un-employed male UK citizen of Pakistani heritage, living in a northern English city, might reasonably and with justification describe him-self in different ways to his parents, to his peers in the locality, to community leaders, to a police officer, to an academic sociologist or to an opinion pollster from the national media. His responses might be different if gathered pre or post the events of 7 July 2005, or if he was asked to identify himself when in a German city or when on a visit to relatives in Pakistan, and so on.

This view of identities – as a palate of pigments from which colours and combinations can be selected at will – is not held by all social scientists. Brubaker and Cooper (2000) argue that identity used to be – and still should be – held in its 'strong' meaning, representing and underlying, the unchanging and long-lasting notion of the self. This was often linked to a strong sense of national identity. They contrast this with what they term 'weak' meanings, which instead stress that individuals have several alternative identities, characterised by a lack of permanence and fluidity. They criticise writers such as Stuart Hall for arguing that identities are used as resources that are employed by the individual to meet their contingent needs, rather than being permanent characteristics.

But Hall is not arguing that all identities are constantly in flux: people generally maintain a fairly constant repertoire of identities, each of which is more or less to the fore in a particular set of social contexts. The individual has but one self, but this is expressed through different identities. These identities are expressed in relationship to others: they are constructed in social contexts and indeed would be meaningless if they were divorced from social settings. A series of classic sociological texts – Berger and Luckman (1966) and Goffman (1969) among others – demonstrate how people present different constructions of themselves to different people with whom they interact. Even what the individual might think to be an intrinsic and natural identity – for example, their sexuality – is determined by social interaction (Foucault, 1978). Implicit in social constructivism is the idea that we can only develop our sense of self-identity through social processes: all our identities are socially determined as we define ourselves in relationship to others, whether in a direct relationship or as the same as or different to the other. Others will also be simultaneously defining our identity in their terms, based on their perceptions and constructions of who they think or assume our identity to be, and this will not always correspond, and may sometimes even be in direct opposition, to the identities we wish to assume.

Jamieson (2002, 2005) extends Hall and Gundara's positions: she uses a social constructionist position to argue that some of these identities are more likely to be 'primary' identities than others, and there are conditions in which some supra-national identities, such as European, are more likely to be primary than local identities. The categorisation of groups and identities is not necessarily always deep and fundamental – putting oneself into a group does not wholly align oneself with all others in the group. In many cases feeling a sense of identity with others may be rather transient. Maylor, Reed, *et al* (2007) explored the identities offered by a wide range of young people in England, and found them offering a variety of ways of describing themselves, offered with varying degrees of confidence. The following examples show an ability to reflect on their heritages:

> pupils regardless of their ethnic background saw themselves as having multiple identities. These identities were derived from the heritage of their parents/other relatives, where they were born and/ or resided, their religion (if they had one), languages spoken (eg Punjabi, Kurdish, Turkish, German, Italian, Patois, French, Finnish, Dari), friendship groups, their personality and in some instances hair/eye/skin colour. (p87)

>> I think of myself as British even though I'm half Irish because it's my parents who are a bit Irish (girl, aged 10)

>> I think I'm a little bit British because I was born here, but my parents were born in Bangladesh (girl, aged 10)

>> I'm not British 'cos my granny's Japanese, my dad was born in Huddersfield and his dad was mostly a lot Scottish, so I'm half Scottish, a third English and a tiny bit Japanese (boy, aged 10)

>> I'm more Geordie because I speak more Geordie words than English (boy, aged 11)

>> I think I am more British because I lived in Scotland until I was 3 and because I go back there – if someone asks me I don't think Scottish or English, I think I am British, the whole of it (girl, aged 14)

>> I'm a bit English, Danish, Spanish, Welsh and Scottish as well (girl, aged 14)

>> I don't know, I'll just say I'm English-German-Irish (boy, aged 15)

>> I was born in England, my Mum's from India and my dad's from here and I'm a Sikh (girl, aged 15)

>> I was born in Russia and I spent half my life there. I'm originally Afghan and I'm a Muslim (girl, aged 15) (Maylor, Read *et al*, 2007, p 87-88)

There was a level of uncertainty amongst some pupils, even if they had lived in Britain for a long time and/or had British parents, whether they were British or not. Some made reference to 'feeling' and 'thinking' British. Similar utterances were made by some non-indigenous pupils who were born in Britain ... From the discussion groups it would seem that pupils living in predominantly White areas are more likely to be vociferous in their articulations of 'British-ness'... some White British pupils [had] the impression that their heritage was not 'different'.

It's boring – I just want to be like from a different race, or quarter, or something (girl, aged 10)

I'm not from a Caribbean country or an exotic country or even France or Spain. I'm from nowhere like that, I'm just plain British (girl, aged 15)

You're bored with it, you're just British (girl, aged 15) (Maylor, Read *et al*, 2007, p96-96)

One of the significant features of the Treaty of Maastricht (European Union, 1992) was the introduction of citizenship of the Union, held by all citizens of member states in the Union. Any citizen of a member state has the right, as a European citizen, to vote and stand for office in local and European elections, and to move between states and live in any one of them. Shore and Black (1994) noted that this had been an aspiration of many who wanted to develop a 'People's Europe', a form of supranational identity. Aspects of this movement include the creation of a common passport, free movement within the Union, and common border controls and a common currency for many of the states. These moves, it was argued, allow the individual European to identify with both the European Union and with their own national state. This multiple nationality, parallel-ing a multiple identity, can be adopted by the individual contingently on their particular position or situation. This is not the only view of European citizenship: the alternative potential for a 'fortress Europe', as exclusive and as chauvinistic as national citizenship can be, is discussed below.

In Chapter Two, Lutz *et al* (2006) were quoted as drawing on extensive Eurobarometer detail to suggest that a growing proportion of young people in the European Community are acknowledging at least a partial sense of European identity, alongside their national identity: the degree to which this is acknowledged varies by nationality, gender and social class, as well as by age. Jenkins (1996) argues that each individual has, within the repertoire of their possible identities, one that is primary, that recognises itself as simultaneously single and inimitable but which also shares some characteristics with particular groups of others. Jenkins follows Berger and Luckman (1966) in identifying particular self-identities as having primacy over others, especially those developed through the interaction of significant others early in life, but these are nevertheless not overwhelming and permanent. This conception of identity, as strong or primary, has often been associated with national identity. Ernest Gellner observed 'a man [*sic*] must have a nationality as he must have a nose and two ears' (Gellner 1983, p6), and Anthony Smith has argued that national identity trumps all others:

> Where once each ethnic community was a world unto itself, the centre of the universe, the light amid darkness, now the heritage and culture values from the storehouse of that same community, selected, reinterpreted and reconstituted, form one unique, incommensurable national identity among many other, equally unique, cultural identities. (Smith 1991, p84)

> Of all the collective identities in which human beings share today, national identity is perhaps the most fundamental and inclusive. ... Other types of collective identity – class, gender, race, religion – may overlap or combine with national identity but they rarely succeed in undermining its hold, though they may influence its direction. (Smith, 1991, p143)

Smith holds that there is 'a straightforward understanding of the concept of 'identity' as 'sameness'. The members of a particular group are alike in just those respects in which they differ from non-members outside the group" (Smith, 1991, p75). But national identity can be analysed as more complex than this. Many writers find Smith's views problematic. To what extent, for example, do all

French citizens see themselves as French? Research about early 20th century France indicates that many rural and provincial inhabitants had little conception of themselves as French (Weber, 1976), while a study of French students in a Paris school in the early 21st century found many of them challenging their presumed incorporation into the republican conception of 'Frenchness' (Mannitz, 2004b). Benedict Anderson (1983, 1991) describes nation state communities as creating identities that were larger than the personal and direct: an imagined political community, imagined as both inherently limited and sovereign. It is imagined because members will never know most of their fellow-members, yet in the minds of each lives the image of their communion. It is limited because it has finite, though elastic boundaries beyond which lie other nations. It is sovereign because it came to maturity at a stage of human history when freedom was a rare and precious ideal. And it is imagined as a community because it is conceived as a deep, horizontal comradeship.

The extent to which these individual imaginations have a common or consistent core is unclear. There are, Anderson observes, various devices and practices that have been followed to foster a sense of joint imagination:

- symbolic events in history, identified to be shared as significant for the nation

- iconic symbols of nationality, from maps and coinage to postage stamps and national airlines

- enactive processes that encourage assimilation and participation in national activities, such as military conscription, the extension of the franchise, participating in national censuses and holidays, and education into a national language, literature and culture.

This combination of the symbolic, iconic and enactive mirrors Bruner's analysis (chapter five, above) of ways of learning, and will be returned to later.

Habermas (1976) suggests that a collective identity, established through such means, can only be understood as a reflexive form: the individual participates in

103

processes of communication in which identity formation occurs as a continuous learning process. Such value and norm creating communications by no means always have the precision of discourses, and they are by no means always institutionalised and therefore to be expected at particular times and places. They often remain diffuse, appear under very different definitions and flow out of the 'base' into the pores of organisationally structured areas of life. They have a subpolitical character, i.e. they operate below the level of political decision processes, but they indirectly influence the political system because they change the normative framework of political decisions. (Habermas, 1976, p116)

In the case of Great Britain, Linda Colley (1992) has shown how the nation was 'forged' (both in the heat of the forge and through the deceit of the forger) through a deliberate process of othering, mercantilism, empire-building and the development of a powerful elite. The essays collected by Hobsbawm and Ranger (1983) illustrate a series of invented traditions that were used to bolster national identities. All these analyses are rather more sceptical of the authenticity and primacy of the nationalism of Smith, with its conception of a deep and shared 'ethnie'.

8

Experiential learning and the young person's construction of identities

How do young people develop their identity? From the previous chapter, it will be clear that the broad answer is through social interaction with others – their family, their peers, and with other social institutions and groups. Being included as a member of such groups will include social interaction about the meaning of the group, its characteristics, the rights and obligations of membership, and the perceived boundaries of the group.

One of the consequences of the belief in the traditions of a national identity, such as those exemplified in Colley's work in Britain in an earlier chapter, was the development of national systems of education. These were often designed as much to reproduce feelings of national identity as they were to sustain national economies (Green, 1990). As Smith observed,

> most governments since the end of the 19th century have seen it as one of their prime duties to establish, fund and increasingly direct a mass system of public education ... in order to create [both] an efficient labour force and [a] loyal, homogeneous citizenry. (Smith, 1995, p91)

School curricula helped generate national and group identity through promulgating national myths and heroes as embodiments of 'national character' (Soysal, 2002, also Schissler and Soysal 2004).

Billig has described these processes as 'banal nationalism', in which nationally propagated 'patterns of social life become habitual or routine ...[and] thoughts, relations and symbols are turned into routine habits, and then become enhabited' (1995, p95). Identity can, from these perspectives of nationalism, be seen to have two distinctive connotations: one of 'being the same as others' and having a continuity with them, and the other being an identity that brings with it the sense of being different from the other.

But the categorisation of groups and identities is not necessarily deep and fundamental in all cases – putting oneself into a group does not in itself mean one feels a fundamental affinity with others who may put themselves in the same group. Although proponents of a strong or fundamental national identity, such as Smith and Gellner, argue that the ascription is more serious, others hold that in many cases the sense of identity or of belonging to a group may be rather evanescent and more transient. They may be particularly temporary in childhood and adolescence.

The processes of schooling often include children creating categories for groups of their peers who become 'the other'. Such distinctions have been observed as based on ethnicity and race (Archer, 2003), gender (Hey, 1997), and on class and sexuality (Mac An Ghaill, 1994). Mannitz describes adolescents of migrant descent in contemporary European schools (London, Berlin, Amsterdam and Paris) as not just understanding such civil conventions but as having

> evidently internalised them and effectively made us of them in their strategies of identity management .... Conceptualisations were negotiated that concerned their own predispositions vis-à-vis the surrounding majority society, together with criteria and views regarding how to asses the presumed cultural differences between their home situations and wider society. ... As well as becoming German, French, Dutch or British, these young people have apparently adopted types of globally marketed youth culture. (Mannitz, 2004a, p308)

The classic 'social identity approach' developed by Tajfel and Turner (1979, Tajfel, 1978, Turner, 1984) recognised that social groups had pre-existing relationships, power and hierarchies and that these social contexts influenced how individuals consequently attributed themselves to a group. This has been critiqued by Widdicombe and Woofitt (1995), who point to evidence that, for young people, social shaping is not always profound: they found that individual adolescents often sought to resist attempts to categorise their identities, claiming that, far from being distinct members of particular youth sub-cultures, they saw themselves as 'normal' and as individuals, and their badges of youth identities were heuristic and casual. Recognising that identities are not always primary can be useful in considering multiple nested identities related to place and territory. The identity of 'national' may be dominant in certain contexts (and in certain periods), but at other times local identities of city or region may become more significant, and supranational identities – such as that of being European, being Muslim, or part of a globalised youth culture – may have greater significance for the individual. Young people will be developing all these identities, adding to their repertoire, from a very early age: and these have an implication for their sense of belonging, and hence for their conception of civic identity (Osler and Starkey, 2003).

Such other, non-national, identities will necessarily be as much imagined communities as Anderson's nations. But they need not be based on a process of othering. While some (such as Rex, 1996a, 1996b) argue that the construction of European identity is equivalent to a new nationalism, based on exclusionism and anti-immigration – despite the Union's rhetoric of anti-racism and anti-xenophobia – others suggest that European identity has little sense of 'the other'. Soysal (2006) points out that there is little that is unique or original in the distinction of the European. Her analysis of European school textbooks identifies the developing presentation of Europe as what she describes as a loose confection that is future-orientated, rather than focused on the past; that does not contrast itself with the other; and that acknowledges that 'European' characteristics of rights, society and welfare are not a monopoly of Europeans.

Citizenship and civil identity can be constructed in terms that do not necessarily relate to national identity. Heater and Oliver (1994) suggested that individuals become citizens when they practice civil virtue and good citizenship, enjoy but do not exploit their civil and political rights, contribute to and receive social and economic benefits, do not allow any sense of national identity to justify discrimination or stereotyping of others, experience a sense of non-exclusive multiple citizenship and, by their example, teach citizenship to others (1994, p 6). This definition does not elaborate the meaning of terms such as civic virtue, but does stress practice and participation. Citizenship is an important aspect of our identities: it is that aspect that involves our political engagement and participation in a community, although Mackenzie has described it as a community associated with a place:

> ... those who share an interest, share an identity; the interest of each requires the collaboration of all. Those who share a place share an identity. *Prima facie* this is a fair statement, whether 'the place' is taken to be 'space-ship earth'; or a beloved land; or a desolate slum or a public housing scheme. (Mackenzie, 1978, p3)

This is not necessarily so: a community can have no spatial characteristics. But Mackenzie is right in asserting that citizenship requires the collaboration of all. In this sense citizenship can be seen as a duty or as an expectation, a necessary part of being a member of the community. For a community to work, the members must have shared experiences.

What are the experiences of children and young people in contemporary Europe which will contribute to their sense of identity? We need first to ask two further questions: what is meant by experience, and what role does experience play in learning?

Experience is a well-used word, with some quite complicated meanings attached to it. John Dewey's definition might be a useful starting point: to him, experience was the 'complex of all which it is distinctively human' (1929, p8), and this was central to education. Education 'might be defined as an emancipation and enlargement of experience' (1933, p340). But the term experience covers both content and process – it includes *what* individuals do and suffer, *what* they struggle for – and also how people act and are acted upon, the ways in which they do and suffer – the processes of *experiencing*. (Dewey, 1929, p8)

Dewey thus distinguished two senses of the word: 'having an experience' and 'knowing an experience'. The 'having' comes from the immediacy of contact with events – primary experience; while 'knowing' is about the interpretation of the event – secondary, or reflective experience (Boud *et al*, 1993, p6; Dewey, 1929, p4). They are thus linked: in a similar manner Michael Oakshott argued that 'experiencing' and 'what is experienced' 'stand to one another in the most complete interdependence; they comprise a single whole' (1933, p9). 'Experience has within it judgment, thought and connectedness with other experience' (Boud *et al*, 1993).

Gilbert Ryle makes a rather similar point when he distinguishes 'knowing that' from 'knowing how'.

> Learning *how* or improving an ability is not like learning that or acquiring information. Truths can be imparted, procedures can only be inculcated, and while inculcation is a gradual process, imparting is relatively sudden. It makes sense to ask at what moment someone became apprised of a truth, but not to ask at what moment someone acquired a skill. (Ryle, 1949, p58)

> A man [*sic*] knowing little or nothing of medical science could not be a good surgeon, but excellence at surgery is not the same thing as knowledge of medical science; nor is it a simple product of it. The surgeon must indeed have learned from instruction, or by his own inductions and observations, a great number of truths; but he must also have learned by practice a great number of aptitudes. (Ryle, 1949, p48-49)

'Learning' can mean quite a wide range of different activities. Säljö (1979) conducted a simple piece of research when he asked adult students what they understood by 'learning'. He identified from this five main categories:

- a quantitative increase in knowledge (acquiring information)

- memorising (storing information to be reproduced)

- acquiring facts, skills, and methods that can be kept and used when needed

- making sense of, or abstracting meaning (relating parts to each other and to the world)

- interpreting and understanding reality (comprehending the world through reinterpreting knowledge)

Ramsden (1992) points out that the last two are qualitatively different. The first three imply a less complex process of learning, that is almost external to the learner – something that just happens or is done to the learner by a teacher. But the final two conceptions concern internalised and personal aspects of learning. It is this kind of learning that is critical for the development of identity – learning that is done in order to understand the real world and in order to act in the real world. Any form of social education that was only the acquisition or memorisation of facts – even interesting or useful information – would be incomplete and unsatisfactory.

The teacher's role should thus be to help students move from just knowing that 'something happened' to *understanding* what the context means. What does it mean in specific relationship to students' identities, their sense of belonging, their identification with a group? How will social experiences create a young citizen who understands and actively participates, be it in a family, a school, a club or a nation? A model of experiential learning developed by David Kolb (1976, 1984) represents experience as a critical element in a cycle or a spiral of experiential learning.

Learning can begin from any one of the four points in this cycle. Often it begins with a person taking some action, and then observing the consequences. Reflecting on these observations leads to the establishment of a rule, or generalisation, or hypothesis – if the action is repeated, then the consequences will be similar. This understanding of a general principle becomes the basis for testing it out in a new context or situation. The new set of concrete experiences may or may not meet the prediction, and thus may need further reflection, and

Figure 8.1: Kolb and Fry's model of experiential learning

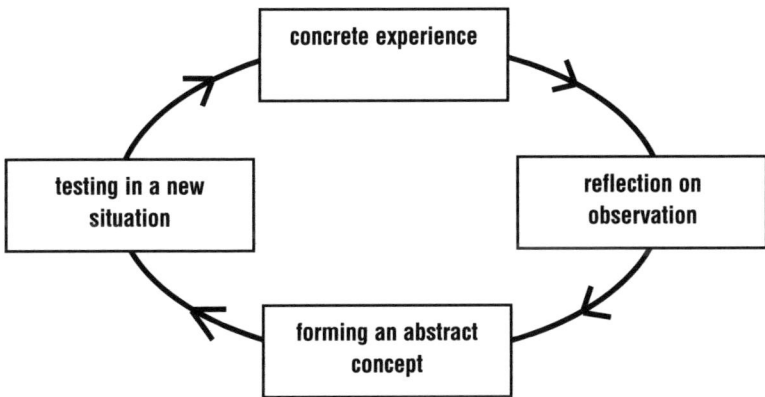

Source: derived from Kolb and Fry, 1985

with this a new concept, or a refining of the original concept. Easton and Dennis (1969) give an example in their study of children and politics. A three and a half year-old boy in the back of the car being driven by his father experiences the car being pulled over by a police officer, and his parent being admonished for speeding. The reflection that follows is that some adults have authority over other adults. Social life is not a simple gerontocracy, where all adults are equal and control children, and the concept that some adults have powers over others may be abstracted from this. This concept is then tested against other experience, and the socio-political concept of authority becomes refined to accommodate generalisations about the range of persons with authority over others, the contexts in which this can be legitimately exercised, the degrees of power that they posses and the sources of these powers, the limitations on them, and so on. This is the process of learning aspects of social and civic identity from experience.

There are two particular aspects of Kolb's model that we should focus on here: immediate experience of social life is used by the learner to test emerging concepts, and the feedback link in the cycle, which the learner uses to change their theories – and their practice.

In the context of citizenship learning, we need to consider the every-day experiences of students and young people, from which their con-ceptualisations will emerge; and what feedback they are likely to get from the behaviour of adults around them, that will support their developing understanding. Kolb draws on Dewey in stressing the developmental nature of this process, and on Piaget in making the link to cognitive development: stressing the role of experience in learning distinguishes this model from simple cognitive theories of learning processes. It also stresses the responsibility that society has for the experiences afforded young people – this learning is not from idealised models of society expressed through texts, but from the here-and-now of lived experience.

Kolb and Fry developed a categorisation of learning styles based on this model. They argued that different individuals have different strengths in learning from particular parts of the cycle: we have dif-ferent levels of ability in using either concrete experiences, reflective observational skills, conceptualisation abilities and experimental abilities. Propensities can be placed on two axes, one ranging from reliance on concrete experience ranging to abstract conceptualisa-tion, the other from reflective observation through to active experi-mentation. These polarities lead to individuals falling into one of four 'learning styles'.

But is this what happens? In terms of citizenship education, what ex-periences of citizenship do young people actually have? There have been a number of criticisms of Kolb's model. It does not help us understand the process of reflection on experiences, though it is useful in helping educators plan learning activities that engage learners (Boud *et al*, 1985). The four styles neatly fit the model, and provide symmetry, but this does not necessarily match reality, and there are some kinds of learning (memorisation) and some kinds of learners (information assimilators) that do not fit (Jarvis, 1987). The model is largely concerned with *individual* learning, what happens in the individual mind: and for social leaning and citizenship educa-tion, as we have seen in chapter six, the *social* processes of learning competitively and cooperatively are key. In particular, the model

Figure 8.2: Four learning styles relating experience, reflection and experimentation

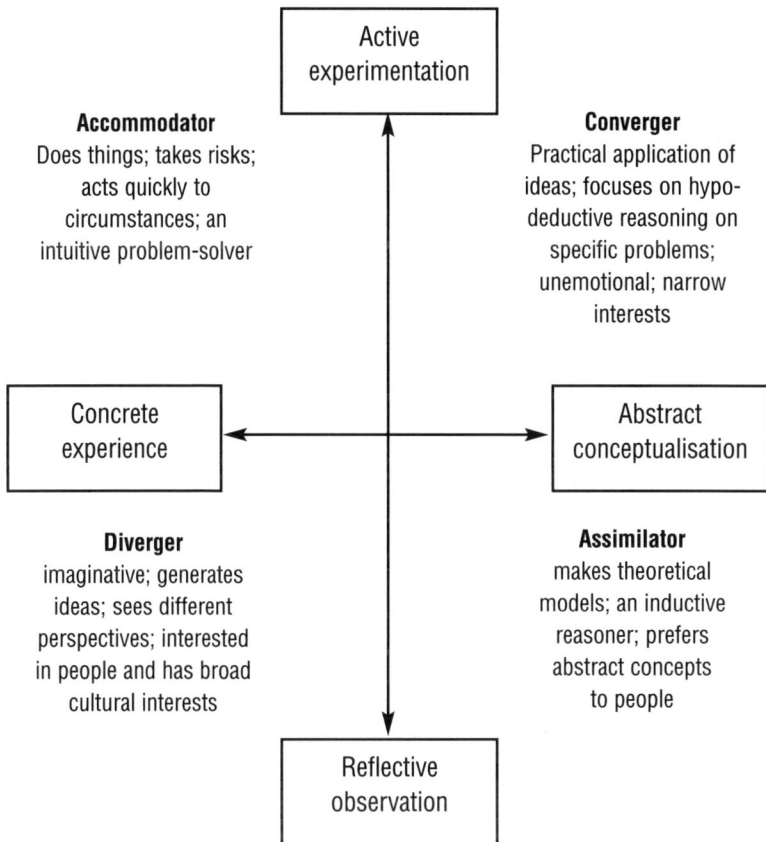

```
                        ┌─────────────────────┐
                        │       Active        │
                        │   experimentation   │
                        └─────────────────────┘
                                   ▲
    Accommodator                   │                    Converger
  Does things; takes risks;        │               Practical application of
      acts quickly to              │                ideas; focuses on hypo-
      circumstances; an            │               deductive reasoning on
   intuitive problem-solver        │                  specific problems;
                                   │                 unemotional; narrow
                                   │                      interests

┌─────────────────┐               │               ┌─────────────────────┐
│    Concrete      │◄──────────────┼──────────────►│      Abstract        │
│   experience     │               │               │  conceptualisation   │
└─────────────────┘               │               └─────────────────────┘

      Diverger                     │                    Assimilator
   imaginative; generates          │                 makes theoretical
   ideas; sees different           │                 models; an inductive
   perspectives; interested        │                 reasoner; prefers
   in people and has broad         │                 abstract concepts
     cultural interests            │                     to people
                                   ▼
                        ┌─────────────────────┐
                        │     Reflective      │
                        │    observation      │
                        └─────────────────────┘
```

Source: derived from Tennant, 1997

does not accommodate different learning conditions and environments, a point returned to below. Do the stages always or inevitably occur in this sequence?

Peter Jarvis (1987, 1995) used Kolb's model to gather empirical data, asking adults explicitly about their own learning styles. From this, he suggested a series of patterns in which experiences of situations resulted on occasions in learning taking place; on other occasions, it did not.

There are many instances where experience does not lead to learning. Some of these may involve some reflection and evaluation, but still result in an active decision not to change one's understanding; other experiences may not even lead to reflection. Experiences do not necessarily lead to reflection, but can nevertheless result in learning: memorisation, for example, or some forms of training. But Jarvis gives particular significance to the forms of reflective learning that Kolb's model suggests. He puts forward three variants:

■ Contemplation, where an experience is reflected on, evaluated, and committed to memory

■ Reflective Practice, in which experience is both reflected on and experimented with, or practiced, often in a cyclical interplay between reasoning and practice, before being committed to memory (rather similar to Schön's 'reflection on and in action')

■ Experiential Learning: experience is turned to an iterative cycle of reasoning and experimentation, before being evaluated and then memorised

This typology offers a more nuanced understanding of experiential learning. There are still problems with stages, because several activities may be happening simultaneously. Nevertheless, what does the model imply about children's and young people's experience of social and civic activity, and how might their identities develop as a consequences of this experience?

In chapter two reference was made to the hidden curriculum in Stan Bowles and Herb Gintis' analysis of the nature of schooling in western capitalist societies (1976, 1980). They looked at both the reasons behind the development of state education, and the practices of schooling found in different kinds of school – elementary, secondary high and state colleges. Schooling, they said, takes place in the form it does to prepare pupils effectively for their future role as workers in a capitalist economy. This preparation is achieved through what they call the 'correspondence principle', where schools' activities and processes correspond to the practices necessary in contemporary production and work. Much of our experience at school is a preparation for our future roles as workers. Capitalist society needs a docile, obedient, motivated workforce – school prepares us for this in three ways:

1. A subservient workforce: those who conform do best at school. Behaving in a compliant and dependable manner is rewarded by being labelled a success, while the child who is aggressive or demonstrates independence is categorised as a failure. At school we learn to obey.

2. Acceptance of hierarchy: those who do what they are told are described as successful learners. Workers lean to follow the boss's orders, because as pupils, they learned to follow the teacher's orders. We are inducted into the hierarchical structures of the workplace through the hierarchy of the school.

3. Motivation by external rewards: pupils are not interested in the subject knowledge they are taught at school, but are encouraged to go to school to get examination passes, an external reward. This is a preparation for the world of work where we do not work for the love of the job, but for the external reward of a wage.

Schools introduce pupils to living their life by the clock, through the school timetable, which is necessary if one is to work regular hours in a factory; they introduce children to uniformity, in dress, behaviour, language and thought – necessary for industry to work efficiently and unquestioningly; they divide knowledge into subjects, much divorced from everyday knowledge and experience – alienating work from experience; they create rewards for achievement in subjects in order to separate and categorise students into hierarchies of obedience – saving employers and universities from considering genuine skills and attributes. Thus what happens at school corresponds to what happens at work. And though Bowles and Gintis developed their analysis and theory specifically around education in capitalist America, their descriptions and findings about the nature and purpose of schooling would apply equally to communist societies.

Bowles and Gintis further argue – this time perhaps specifically in a capitalist context – that achievement in school and a pupil's life chances are determined to a great extent by their class. Conformity leads to the working patterns necessary for an industrialised society; achievement in school relates to social class orientation that can be passed off as meritocracy, allowing those of a higher social class to be licensed, through more advanced and higher education, into the work patterns and pseudo-independence of the professions and academia (see also Coles, 1988).

If this analysis is accepted, what experience of social and civic identity would be provided by schools in such systems? Students would learn about obedience to authority; the acceptance of (possibly arbitrary) imposed rules; the division of society into ranks; and the acknowledgement of hierarchy. Cultural norms are essentialised. Individual identity is sacrificed to institutional conformity.

What kind of experiences of citizenship do our educational institutions – nurseries, schools and universities – actually provide? The consequence of experiential learning is that people learn from their environment and experience, and that what young people will be learning from non-democratic institutions, from un-civil learning establishments, will be non-democratic and uncivil patterns of behaviour. Moreover, if at the same time we are teaching, in the formal curriculum, a different set of messages about democratic values and the norms of civilisation, it would not be surprising if young people were cynical about the political process, apathetic in their civic participation, and generally contributing to the growth of the democratic deficit.

There are alternative scenarios. One of the most interesting analyses of the past decade has been the notion of learning through legitimate peripheral participation in learning communities. The idea of situated learning, developed by social anthropologist Jean Lave and former teacher Etienne Wenger, stresses that learning is social, that it comes about through participation in everyday life, and that it is continuous through life. This has important implications for the acquisition of identities, and for the institutions needed to foster their development.

Wenger argues that there is a widespread supposition that learning is an individual activity. Schools, although they are social settings, in practice generally strive to develop the *individual's* abilities and understanding through teaching practices, assessment techniques, and reporting procedures, all of which assume that it is the individual who 'learns'. Learning is generally supposed to have 'a beginning and an end; that it is best separated from the rest of our activities; and that it is the result of teaching' (Wenger 1998, p3). Lave suggests that we should reconceptualise the relationship between learning, educational institutions and learners as a social process. *Situated Learning: Legitimate peripheral participation* (Lave and Wenger, 1991) proposed their core ideas, followed up by further works (such as Lave and Chaiklin, 1993 and Wenger, 1998). Their work does not draw on experiences in schools, but is about apprenticeship in informal learning institutions – for example, among Yucatec midwives in Central America, Vai and Gola tailors in West Africa, US Navy quartermasters, and non-drinking alcoholics in Alcoholics Anonymous. How do the identities of these initiates develop so that they become accepted members of these groups? Their ideas have been moved on to situations of formal schooling more recently by Barbara Rogoff (1990).

Lave and Wenger argue that communities of practice are ubiquitous, and that most people are involved in a number of them, at work, school, home, or at leisure. Human beings are constantly engaged in the pursuit of enterprises of all kinds: as we define and pursue these in social groups, we interact with each other and with the environment, and change or fine-tune our relations with each other ...

> in other words, we learn. Over time, this collective learning results in practices that reflect both the pursuit of our enterprises and the attendant social relations. These practices are thus the property of a kind of community created over time by the sustained pursuit of a shared enterprise. It makes sense, therefore to call these kinds of association *communities of practice*. (Wenger, 1998, p45)

Communities of practice have varied procedures and habits, from the formal to the informal, but in each of these members are joined through common activities and by what they have learned through their mutual engagement in these activities. They have shared identities. Wenger proposed that communities of practice define themselves in three ways:

- by their joint nature and purpose, which is always being renegotiated by members through their practice

- by their functioning, and they way that members knit a social entity together

- by their production of a shared repertoire of resources – whether these are routines, vocabularies, common understandings and beliefs (Wenger, 1999).

This is not the simple acquisition of skills and knowledge for a task, but the establishment of relationships and communities with a sense of joint enterprise and identity, with a shared set of ideas and commitments, and shared resources: it is about ways of doing and approaching things that are shared to some significant extent among members. The relationship of this to citizenship, and to civic behaviour, is evident. Citizenship is above all a community of practice, rather than a simple set of structures and knowledge. Lave and Wenger thus are focusing on everyday experiences of being members of groups, and the informal experiential learning that creates a community of practice. They are coming at experiential leaning from a different – and more revealing – direction than that taken by Kolb and Jarvis. As Hanks puts it in his introduction to their book:

> Rather than asking what kind of cognitive processes and conceptual structures are involved, they ask what kinds of social engagements provide the proper context for learning to take place. (Lave and Wenger, 1991, p14)

This idea of a kind of apprenticeship is not learners acquiring a model of the world, but of learners participating in a community that has a model of the world – 'being active participants in the *practices* of social communities and constructing *identities* in relation to these communities' (Wenger 1998, p4).

118

A learner will incrementally gather knowledge through this informal apprenticeship, simply through being with people who are expert and thus have more knowledge. Lave and Wenger illustrate this happening with novice midwives, tailors and quartermasters gradually acquiring expert knowledge and skills. Since then, other studies have looked at the contribution of informal learning to the development of professional knowledge in, for example, engineering, medicine, law and in community workers (Gear, McIntosh and Squires, 1994; Cullen *et al*, 1999), or in another study, how Brazilian carpenters with little formal education manage to build a much better understanding of the mathematical ideas related to their carpentry through informal relationships than carpenters enrolled in formal apprenticeship classes that teach the same ideas (Carraher and Schliemann, 2000).

There is a sequence in this. People begin by joining or becoming part of a community and learning at the periphery. As their competence develops, they move towards the centre of the community. Learning is not the acquisition of knowledge by an individual, but the process of *social* participation, and the situation defines the process:

> The mastery of knowledge and skill requires newcomers to move toward full participation in the socio-cultural practices of a community. 'Legitimate peripheral participation' provides a way to speak about the relations between newcomers and old-timers, and about activities, identities, artefacts, and communities of knowledge and practice. A person's intentions to learn are engaged and the meaning of learning is configured through the process of becoming a full participant in a socio-cultural practice. This social process, includes, indeed it subsumes, the learning of knowledgeable skills. (Lave and Wenger, 1991, p29)

Lave and Wenger are advocating a more complex idea of relating experience to learning. 'For newcomers, the purpose is not to learn *from* talk as a substitute for legitimate peripheral participation; it is to learn *to* talk as a key to legitimate peripheral participation' (Lave and Wenger, 1991, p108-9). There are two key corollaries: knowledge cannot be abstract or out of context; and new learning occurs in the community of practice (Tennant, 1997). These may not always be true.

Barbara Rogoff has shown how this kind of *Apprenticeship in Thinking* (1990) is a social activity that requires 'guided participation' from more experienced practitioners, and that this can be found in the way that young children learn about their social environment. For example, many children will, by the time they reach the stage of formal schooling, already have some familiarity with print from sources such as the sides of buses, advertising and the like – as well as from books. In their seminal comparison of four year olds informal learning at home with their learning in nursery class, Tizard and Hughes (1984) found that, irrespective of social class, that the mother-child relationship provided a rich informal learning environment:

> ... the most frequent learning context was that of everyday living. Simply by being around their mothers, talking, arguing and endlessly asking questions, the children were being provided with large amounts of information relevant to growing up in our culture. (Tizard and Hughes, 1984, p250-251)

On the other hand, the Nursery class, despite its informal approach was quite different:

> The questioning, puzzling child we were so taken with at home was gone ... conversations with adults were mainly restricted to answering questions rather than asking them, or taking part in minimal exchanges... (Tizard and Hughes, 1984, p9)

Rogoff has taken Lave and Wenger's ideas to incorporate her own work on guided apprenticeship in school settings. She describes practice in an innovative school in Salt Lake City, where teachers, students and parents work together on the basis that 'learning occurs through interested participation with other learners' (Rogoff *et al*, 2001). And more recently, in *The Cultural Nature of Human Development* (2003), she draws attention to the need to examine the cultural processes that shape children's development, rather than simply focusing on determining when children can accomplish particular skills. All children grow as members of cultural communities, so understanding how childhood is supported, constrained, and constructed in any community is a significant part of understanding child development and learning. Legitimate peripheral participation and the idea of a community of practice has three particular areas of significance for learning about citizenship in a meaningful way, and the experience of citizenship that society and its institutions needs to provide for young people.

Firstly, learning about citizenship is embedded in relationships between people, within a community of practice. What kind of democratic relationships exist in our learning institutions that constitute practice? Bowles and Gintis (1976) suggest that the school context is negative, authoritarian and anti-democratic. In the introduction to Patricia Murphy's book *Learners, Learning and Assessment* (1999), McDermott points out that

> Learning traditionally gets measured on the assumption that it is a possession of individuals that can be found inside their heads... [but] learning is in the relationships between people .... Learning does not belong to individual persons, but to the various conversations of which they are a part. (in Murphy, 1999, p17)

Practicing citizenship, taking part – first tentatively on the margins, and then with increasing confidence, with mounting fluency and control – critically depends on being able to take part in a set of relationships that demonstrate and substantiate democratic civic values and practices. Without these relationships, without this participation, the culture of citizenship will not flourish, will not even start.

Secondly, it is the responsibility of the teachers in educational institutions to enable participation in the community of practice. We need to consider how we both legitimate and ensure access for all students to be able to collaborate in the dialogue. In the Salt Lake City school, Barbara Rogoff observed that the teachers gave precedence to 'instruction that builds on children's interests in a collaborative way ...learning activities are planned by children as well as adults, and where parents and teachers not only foster children's learning but also learn from their own involvement with children' (2001, p3). This in itself is a model of socio-political education, developing a community of respect for the learner and for the group,

121

for relating the priorities of the individual to those of the group, and for identifying rights, duties and obligations. It is also a vehicle for the exercise of the skills of citizenship: recognition of others, reasoning, argument, debate and resolution.

Finally, there is a central and critical relationship between knowledge about citizenship and 'doing citizenship' – the practice and experience of citizenship. Situated learning for democracy requires learning to be situated in democratic practice. We need to think carefully about what we mean by practice, and how this bears on knowledge. Education in this sense requires both informed action and action with a direction of purpose.

9

Citizenship and the development of rights

Citizenship is one of our identities, but it is not solely an identity. Nor are all citizenships the same: the identity of a citizen of the Third Reich, for example, would involve a qualitatively different identity to a citizen of contemporary Cuba, or a to a citizen of Europe. W J M Mackenzie's observation, cited in the previous chapter, suggested that citizenship is associated with a shared identity focusing on a sense of place (Mackenzie, 1978). Members must participate. Involvement or participation is an active state – it is not merely accepting a label, assenting to be a part of something. It is something that everyone should do: it is a communal activity, not just a spectator activity, and certainly not an elite pursuit. Asserting that there is a duty or obligation to participate may be too emphatic, but it is nevertheless reasonable to have an expectation that the great majority, if not all, citizens in a democratic society should participate in civic affairs. Such expectations, or duties, bring with them the corollary of the individual having rights in the society. This chapter will explore the relationship between rights and citizenship. It will argue that this relationship is particularly important in the context of education and learning, for two reasons.

Firstly European citizenship, as has been argued in chapter six, is peculiarly centred on the rights of the citizen. The supranational and binding nature of the European Charter on Human Rights is a unique empowerment of the citizen.

Secondly, the development of rights gives a potent learning ground for the development of active citizenship. Learning about rights already achieved is important and is an appreciation of those who won those rights for us to enjoy today, but enactive learning of active citizenship can be developed particularly well in examining the extension of rights to new areas.

There are three particular categorisations of rights in relationship to citizenship that will be drawn on in the following argument: the work of T H Marshall in the late 1940s, Karel Vasak in the late 1970s, and John Urry in the 1990s.

Marshall (1950) suggested that citizenship is essentially about the establishment and the exercise of rights. Citizenship was a process of belonging to a political entity that gave its members the protection of particular rights. Rights are intrinsically defined by citizenship: as Montero puts it, 'The defining and primordial element of citizenship is the enjoyment of political rights' (1992, p1140).

The idea that all people have rights is a relatively new concept. Thomas Hobbes, writing in the 17th century, said that without civil government the life of people was 'solitary, poor, nasty, brutish, and short' (1651, Ch 13), but that nevertheless, people are born with rights: the rights to life and liberty (Ch 14). John Locke added to this the right to property. In his *Second Treatise on Government* (1690, Ch 5) he argued that natural law begins and ends with the natural right of property: the purpose of civil government was to protect property and the right of property.

Traditionally, these rights were granted by a nation state, and Hobbes, Locke and others devised explanations of how civil society was a contractual relationship between people, who agreed to join together to create systems of person-made law (as opposed to divinely revealed law) that guaranteed particular rights – of liberty, property, political participation and freedom of expression. What made these two political philosophers distinctive and original, compared with the prevalent orthodoxy of their times, was their insistence that these rights were dependant – unlike the absolutism or divine right that had characterised political authority up this point – on the consent of the people. These rights were socially constructed.

Marshall suggested that there had been three stages in the development of rights – citizenship first gave civil rights in the eighteenth century, then political rights in the nineteenth century, and thirdly social rights in the twentieth century. Civil rights included the right to property, privacy, and to freedom of expression; political rights extended voting rights from the richer male property owners to the poor and to women; and social rights included the right of access to education, health care, social security.

Elements of the early definitions of civil rights, devised by contract philosophers such as Hobbes and Locke, were incorporated in the English Bill of Rights of 1689, which set out the conditions of parliament for the invitation to William of Orange to become a constitutional monarch: the king had to acknowledge the right of Parliament (and not of the King) to make and enforce laws, raise taxes and maintain an army, and that elections to Parliament should be free, its meetings frequent, and its proceedings free from interference.

The American Declaration of Independence nearly ninety years later spelt these rights out with greater clarity:

> .. all men are created equal, that they are endowed by their Creator with certain inalienable rights, that among these are life, liberty and the pursuit of happiness. That to secure these rights, governments are instituted among men, deriving their just powers from the consent of the governed. (United States, 1776)

Government is designed and empowered to secure rights, and the power to do this is based on assent. Following the French Revolution, the French National Assembly adopted the Declaration of the Rights of Man and the Citizen in 1797. This was consciously modelled on the United States Declaration, and probably drafted partly by Mirabeau (who had written *'Toute l'Europe a applaudi au sublime manifeste des États-Unis d'Amérique'* (1782), and partly by Lafayette.

The French Declaration lists additional rights: the right to resist oppression, the right to have officials responsible to the public, and freedom was defined as 'the power to do anything which does not harm another: therefore, the only limits to the exercise of each person's natural rights are those which ensure that the other members of the community enjoy those same rights'.

These rights – in France, England and the USA – were not uniformly upheld at the time, or subsequently, even in those three countries, who were then in the van of the establishment and codification of rights. In particular, slavery, colonisation and the treatment of indigenous populations were not seen as subject to these rights. Women were rarely seen as included in statements of rights. Other countries began to adopt similar statements of rights in the century that followed, but often with limited applicability. For example, the 1815 Congress of Vienna, held by the states that had defeated Napoleon, condemned the slave trade as inconsistent with human rights, but did little to acknowledge the demands for greater democracy and self-determination. It was only gradually that these kinds of rights came to be seen as universal.

But these were only the first stage of Marshall's trilogy of human rights. His next two stages, political and social rights, followed in many parts of the world. The Czech jurist Karel Vasak has proposed dividing human rights into three generations, divided according to the watchwords of the French Revolution: *Liberté, Égalité, Fraternité.* These in many ways extend Marshall's division (Vasak, 1979/ 1982).

First generation human rights concern liberty. They are civil and political in nature, protecting the individual from the state. They include freedom of speech, the right to a fair trial, and freedom of religion. They are largely *negative* rights, prohibiting the state or others from exercising certain constraints over the individual, and are seen at the global level in the example of the Universal Declaration of Human Rights (United Nations, 1948): they summate Marshall's first two waves of rights, the civil and the political.

Vasek's second generation human rights concern equality, and are essentially social, economic and cultural in nature. They should lead to different citizens having equivalent or similar conditions and treatment, the right to work and to be employed, and thus the ability to support a family. These are largely *positive* rights – things the State should provide for its people. Some of these are found in Articles 22 to 27 of the Universal Declaration: more are detailed in the International Covenant on Economic, Social, and Cultural Rights (United Nations, 1966). This range of rights is, very broadly, equivalent to Marshall's third wave of social rights.

Third generation human rights concern fraternity and solidarity, and focus on the rights an individual has as a claim upon society. Vasek suggests that generally this third generation has not yet been addressed in any binding human rights agreement, but we are now extending our idea of rights yet further. The third writer on rights to be introduced is John Urry (1995), who suggests six new categories of rights:

■ Cultural citizenship – each culture has the right to preserve its identity

■ Minority citizenship – minorities have rights to reside in and remain in other societies, and have as full rights as the dominant group

■ Ecological citizenship – the right to live in a sustainable environment

■ Cosmopolitan citizenship – everyone has the right to relate to other citizens, cultures and societies without state inter-ference

■ Consumer citizenship – the rights to open access to goods, services and information

■ Mobility citizenship – the rights of visitors and tourists moving through other countries and societies (Urry, 1995).

What is also changing are ideas about who makes and grants these rights. In its original sense, citizenship was membership of a politi-cal community which brought with it rights to political participation, and certain duties. The traditional rights of citizenship came about

Figure 9.1: The relationships between the categories of rights proposed by Marshall, Vasak and Urry

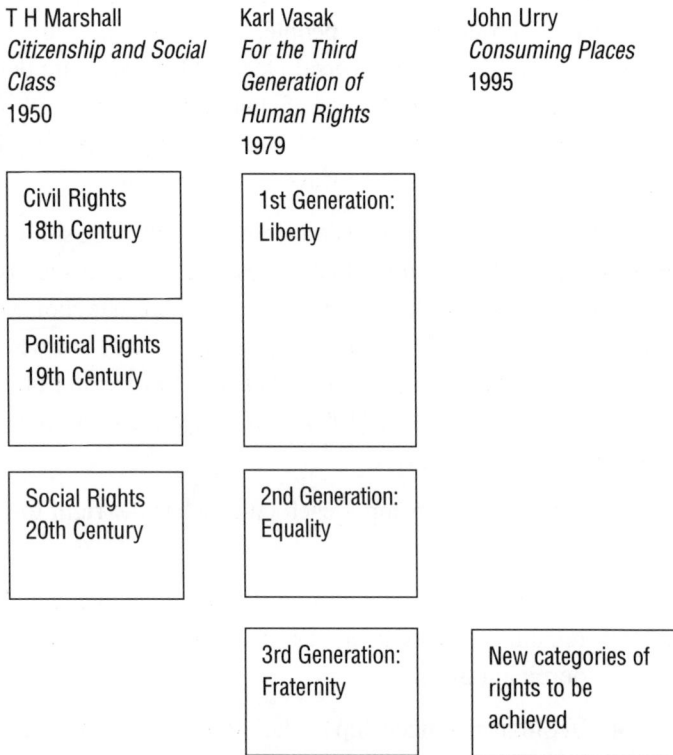

T H Marshall
Citizenship and Social Class
1950

Karl Vasak
For the Third Generation of Human Rights
1979

John Urry
Consuming Places
1995

Civil Rights 18th Century	1st Generation: Liberty	
Political Rights 19th Century		
Social Rights 20th Century	2nd Generation: Equality	
	3rd Generation: Fraternity	New categories of rights to be achieved

by being members of a sovereign state – a process that started in Europe with the Treaty of Westphalia in 1648 (see chapter three) and the absolute sovereignty of the nation state. But this sovereignty has become eroded and challenged, particularly over the past 60 years. The state's right to grant citizenship and to rule over what rights citizens have has been fragmented. This has come about in a variety of ways: one example is the erosion of the monopoly over the granting of citizenship, allowing the possibility of dual or multiple citizenship to grow. Certain rights have been placed above the nation state, or at least, an attempt to do so has been made: for example, the Universal Declaration of Human Rights places a moral obligation on signatory states to respect greater rights. Much more significantly, the European Convention on Human Rights (Council of Europe, 1950) creates legal rights for Europeans that are superior and enforceable above the state level. The European Court of Human Rights and the European Court of Justice have judicial powers that surpass those of the member states. This has broken the link between human rights and the territory of the nation state. Political and other rights are being given and guaranteed by a body greater than the nation state. This is 'a new model of membership, anchored in the deterritorialised notions of person rights' (Soysal, 1997, p3).

These new forms of citizenship uncouple rights from territory. This can be confusing: Urry feels that 'there is an increasing contradiction between rights, which are universal, uniform and globally defined, and social identities, which are particularistic and territorially specified' (Urry, 1999, p312).

The European Union's Charter of Fundamental Rights of the European Union (European Union, 2000a) includes precepts concerning democratic forms of government, and of the rights of citizens, which members of the Union enforce through their own law and through the European Human Rights court in Strasbourg. Significantly, these definitions are extended beyond the boundaries of the European Union, in that nations seeking to join the Union must demonstrate their adherence to the precepts of the European Convention, and countries seeking trade and other bilateral agreements with the Union are, through the Cotonou Agreement, expected to include human rights agreements.

Active citizenship requires that individuals work to develop the community they live in through participation, volunteer work and efforts to improve life for all citizens. This is not the same as the older legal definition of citizenship, which was passive, narrower, territorial and specifically related to allegiance to the government of a state, and probably related to nationality. In the context of citizenship education, these new dimensions and comprehensions of citizenship are critical: if we were to confine education to consider only legal national citizenship, all that would be needed would be a narrow description of the methods of acquiring citizenship – *jus sanguinis versus jus solis* – and a listing of formal rights and duties. But the broader definition requires some active consideration of community 'political community' can be any grouping that has a political agenda, meaning any group involved in seeking or maintaining support for some public or common action. In this sense, politics is observed in all human group interactions including corporate, academic, and religious interactions, and not simply in governments.

Citizenship is about the construction of a community of rights. This community can be a nation state, the European community, or much smaller – for example, a school. The nature of citizenship essentially concerns the establishment of rights, and the changing and extending nature of these rights. These rights have become separated from the entities of the nation-state. There are three ways in which citizenship is disseminated, as noted by Anderson (1991) – through symbolic icons such as flags, anthems, airlines, state regalia and pageantry; through abstract conceptions such as legal norms and principles; and through active participation as citizens. Anderson's analysis helps us to address questions such as how should pre-schools, schools, colleges and universities disseminate ideas of citizenship to students and learners, and what is entailed in teaching this sort of citizenship.

Jerome Bruner's *Theory of Instruction* (1966a) was introduced in chapter five. He advocated three 'ways of knowing', through action, through imagery, and through the medium of symbols. His three modes of knowing correspond to the three ways in which citizenship is disseminated and rights are understood. Bruner's principle for teaching and learning is that the combination of concrete, pictorial and symbolic activities is the most effective.

Studies of socio-political learning in many societies show that young children rapidly pick up iconic forms of the nation state and the community: research shows that American 6 year-olds recognise the flag, the presidency, the White House and Congress; and then, later in their schooling, are introduced to the symbolic or conceptual representation, through civics lessons that describe the structures and processes, and the list of rights and duties (Easton and Dennis,

1969; Greenstein, 1965; Connell, 1971; Hess and Torney, 1967). But these reports rarely identify enactive forms of citizenship education. Abstract learning occurs in formal teaching processes and courses, perhaps particularly in history. Enactive learning presents new and greater prospects. How can teachers translate citizenship into enactive forms?

One possible way is through children and young people being aware of situations in which rights are denied. There are many places where regimes do not recognise the rights of various groups of the population, or indeed any of the population. Young people are often actively engaged in work with organisations such as Amnesty International, in lobbying and demanding the rights of others. The importance of these newer rights is that they give opportunities for young people to work actively to achieve in citizenship activities, rather than passively learning about or being taught about rights won in the past. In the post-national model of society and education suggested by Davies *et al* (2005; also Davies 2006) there is an emphasis on the external focus, on extra-national perspectives and identities, and on the civic inclusion of those who historically have been excluded.

But a more general and personal approach would be through recognising that there are further rights to be obtained. Returning to Karel Vasak's 'three generations of rights', we are reminded that the third generation is largely yet to be won. This third generation involves fraternity and solidarity, the rights an individual may claim from society. John Urry's list of six new categories may suggest areas in which children and young people, as well as adults, might become actively involved in arguing for and establishing new rights. Because it is in arguing for and achieving that enactive learning about rights will occur.

Indeed, many young people are engaged in these areas:

- Cultural citizenship, where there is wide interest in, and sympathy for, the rights of diverse cultural groups, particularly in the face of globalisation; and where there are many successful attempts to preserve cultures and languages. A rights agenda may well develop here.

■ Minority citizenship, where questions of asylum, settlement and migration are not necessarily knee-jerk reactions, particularly among many young people. International conventions on refugees are under attack, and many young people are interested in actively defending and possibly extending these rights.

■ Ecological citizenship is a particular potent area that resonates deeply with young people. The right to live in a sustainable environment seems particularly interesting to the young, and is an area of active participation and active learning.

■ Cosmopolitan citizenship is again an area in which young people are active in many situations. Relationships across cultural and ethnic differences are increasing, in some places very rapidly; yet in others are held back. The rights to relate to other citizens, cultures and societies without state interference is another area for activity.

■ Consumer citizenship has a wide range of meanings: it is not merely about being an informed purchaser, but an active decision maker and actively demanding consumer rights and responsibilities: curtailing the power of producers to exploit consumers, and to exploit workers and natural resources.

■ Mobility citizenship, the rights of visitors and tourists moving through other countries and societies.

The argument is, therefore, that enactive learning of citizenship will naturally involve the enactive engagement in the extension of rights. This will not be about the study and appreciation of rights that have been achieved, or the icons and concepts that relate to these, but the involvement of young people in establishing rights in their own schools and societies, and extending rights to the third generation. Teaching Citizenship is learning citizenship through participation.

10

Educational practice and the development of rights and active citizenship

The previous chapter examined the nature of citizenship, its relationship to the establishment of rights, and the changing and extending nature of these rights. These rights have become separated from the entities of the nation state, and consequently from the ways in which nation states and supra-national communities establish identities, citizenship and rights. In particular, it was suggested that there are three ways in which citizens' rights are disseminated – through symbolic icons, through abstract conceptions, and through active participation. The questions that follow for the educator are how should our pre-schools, schools, colleges and universities disseminate these ideas of citizenship to their students and learners? What does teaching this sort of citizenship entail?

Earlier chapters argued that citizenship has powerful links with identity and rights, both of which have been strongly associated with territory and nation. These two areas have become increasingly complex and contested, and this complexity provides fertile ground for young people to explore what citizenship means in an active and participatory manner.

Rights-based citizenship may be particularly relevant, especially the developing waves of new areas of human rights described by Vasak and Urry. Many young people are actively concerned with and engaged in these issues, and the development of supra-national rights also raises issues of sovereignty and of identity. The complex relationship between rights, identity and citizenship can be debated in a variety of contexts – local and national and other – and conceptions of citizenship can be discussed. When children and young people become aware of situations in which rights which they enjoy are denied to others, they often actively engage in work with lobbying groups and non-governmental organisations in pushing for and demanding rights for others.

Chapter four distinguished between learning for active citizenship and learning for passive citizenship, showing a strong preference for the former. It was argued that citizenship education needs to address values and dispositions, skills and competencies, and knowledge and understanding; and that issues of identity and rights should be at the heart of the content of a citizenship education programme. How do we combine these into a realistic curricular programme for a school or other educational institution? To offer some suggestions I draw extensively on the useful analysis undertaken by Deakin Crick and her colleagues (2004) in a meta-review of recent research on the practice of citizenship education in the UK.

These analyses of the citizenship curriculum suggest four key areas for the planning and delivery of effective learning. These constitute a package – they are closely related to each other and interdependent, not a shopping list from which a selection might be made. They are

- facilitating classroom discourse and a dialogic pedagogy in the classroom

- a concomitant valuing and respect for the student and their experiences, as a partner in citizenship learning

- a coherent and radical construction of the school as a democratic institution that accords genuine rights and responsibilities to all its members

- a structure to support teachers and other staff to engage in these processes

Deakin Crick's first set of principles suggest that the quality of dialogue and discourse is central: this is essential to allow pupils to identify and share values and rights, and in allowing them to construct concepts of justice and equality cooperatively. Higher order critical and creative thinking skills depend on the processes of learning, the quality of pupil-teacher and pupil-pupil relationships and on the dialogue associated with these relationships. Such a facilitative and conversational pedagogy will require a re-ordering of the traditional power and authority structures of the school, and necessitate an inclusive and respectful quality to teacher-pupil relationships.

This leads to a second group of principles: the empowerment of the pupil voice, and the space and opportunity for them to articulate and construct meaning from their life experiences and identities. The use of pupils' contextual knowledge in a problem-solving context will lead to citizenship engagement and action. The classroom teacher and the whole school staff need to make opportunities to engage with the values embedded in all subjects, across the curriculum, but that also demonstrably linked to pupils' lives and personal narratives.

This in turn implies the whole school adopting a strategy that defines itself as exemplifying, , community values that define it as a democratic and respectful institution in all its practices. Such a strategy not only requires powerful leadership, but also needs to involve every member of the school community. Educational establishments need structures that allow participation and democratic processes to be the core, and this puts particular demands on the skills and attitudes of all members of the community, pupils and staff. Citizenship education is not a bolt-on activity to be transmitted by a small group of staff in isolation from the rest of the school. The student voice needs not merely to be listened to, but to be trusted and honoured.

Finally, this process requires the establishment of support for teachers and other school staff to develop their professional skills to accomplish these classroom and whole school transformations.

Figure 10.1: Active citizenship in the school and a willingness to prioritise citizenship within the curriculum

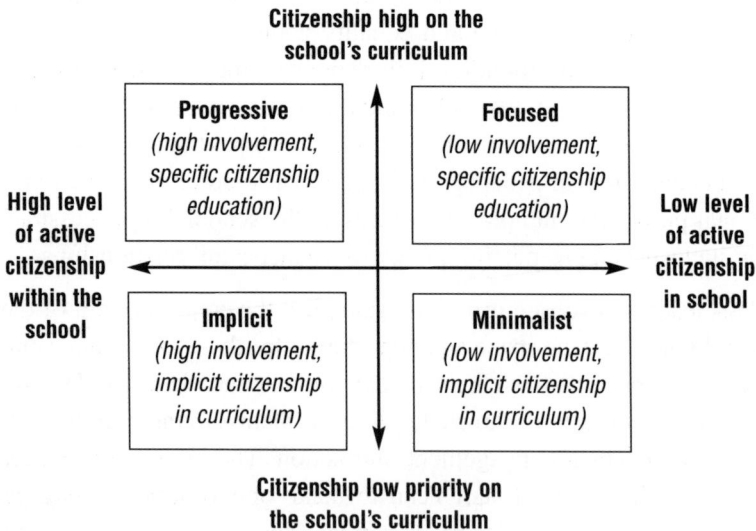

Citizenship high on the
school's curriculum

		Progressive *(high involvement,* *specific citizenship* *education)*		Focused *(low involvement,* *specific citizenship* *education)*	

High level
of active
citizenship
within the
school

Low level
of active
citizenship
in school

| Implicit
(high involvement,
implicit citizenship
in curriculum) | Minimalist
(low involvement,
implicit citizenship
in curriculum) |

Citizenship low priority on
the school's curriculum

Source: after Ireland *et al*, 2006

The last two sections of this chapter draw particularly on this experience and practice and explore these transformations in greater detail, at the whole school and at the classroom level.

There have been a number of attempts to classify how schools have approached the organisation of citizenship education. One of the largest studies, undertaken by the UK's National Foundation for Educational Research (NFER), is a longitudinal study (still in progress) of how English secondary schools have implemented citizenship education as a new national curriculum subject (see, for example, Ireland *et al*, 2006). This study offers a largely descriptive model of the extent of school engagement with the subject, based on a simple two-dimensional matrix.

One scale represents greater or lesser involvement in active citizenship in the school and community, the other a general willingness to forefront citizenship education within the curriculum. Schools thus are classified into four types: progressive (high involvement, speci-

136

fic citizenship education), focused (low involvement, specific citizenship education), implicit (high involvement, implicit citizenship) and minimalist (low involvement and implicit citizenship).

However, this does not really help us understand what kind of school ethos is necessary for effective learning, and why. Rather more useful is McGettrick's (2002) review of how teacher educators approach citizenship, in which three broad approaches were identified. In the transmission approach there was a focus on knowledge and content of citizenship, with a traditional instructional style, a focused methodology, and an inflexible programme design. The process approach was centred on the context of schooling and how schooling was organised: this was characterised by developmental teaching, varied methodologies and flexible programme design. McGettrick's third, and preferred, approach was of professional transformational, in which teachers become re-professionalised as facilitators, focusing on learning for transforming society. The teacher is seen as a primary agent of social change working in the context of a community.

This approach is articulated most clearly in the case study of a school undertaken by Deakin Crick (2002). She describes how a carefully planned whole-school intervention in the structuring and delivery of spiritual, moral and cultural education was able to change the way pupils saw and articulated the core values of school. These values were not transmitted through distinct lessons in the conventional manner, but underpinned the whole school approach to teaching and learning. All teachers were involved in the identification of nine core values, such as valuing oneself and others, justice, forgiveness, truth and trust, and all agreed to their implementation. Curriculum planning followed on from this, and Deakin Crick tracked how these changes were introduced over two terms. She identifies that in addition to this 'whole school, whole person' approach, the quality of student thinking and talking in the classroom was critically important, and that the value of such high quality discourse could not be understated.

Such an approach requires a high degree of consultation within a school, at all levels. This is shown in a study of the introduction of citizenship education in Western Australia (Criddle, 2004), where he noted that, at the state level, it was particularly important that government agencies recognised teachers' professional identities when they sought to introduce major changes to teaching approaches.

Most schools are less committed to such a root and branch revision. A study described by Leighton (2004) found that many teachers assumed that they were already naturally democratic: they fell into a syllogistic trap that 'democracy is good, we are democratic, therefore we are good', without considering what democratic meant in the practice of the school. Consequently there was often a contradiction between the stated ethos of a school and its practices: he noted that this cognitive dissonance, clearly identified by students, did 'not appear to depress or alienate the young so much as disinterest them' (Leighton, 2004, p179).

There are examples of less radical whole school approaches than that described by Deakin Crick. For example, Sliwka (2006) describes substantial deliberative projects in some German secondary schools, involving whole schools considering an issue over a several non-consecutive days with the participation of politicians and others. More common is the introduction of schools councils. These can provide valuable lessons in different systems of voting. In exploring various forms of alternative voting patterns with 10 year-olds as they elected two classroom representatives, we managed to demonstrate the different results between first past the post systems and alternative transferable voting: this lead to an exploration of constituencies and gerrymandering. The evidence of the effectiveness of schools councils in bringing about active citizenship is mixed. A study by Flecknoe (2002) found that pupils appreciated how councils enabled pupils to be listened to, which lead to an increase in self-confidence, in decision making abilities, cooperation, and in conflict resolution.

> The overall impression from these conversations with the pupils, and from their pictures, is that they consider the school council to be important; it gives them opportunity to speak and be heard; it is a pleasant experience; important items are discussed; the school

and governors all take this seriously; decisions are taken in a non-threatening way, by consensus; they have an understanding of aspects of democracy in action. (Flecknoe, 2002, p435)

Flecknoe warned that both pupils and staff needed to be supported concurrently in developing these skills, and that to be successful democratic participation had to centre around real topics rather than peripheral issues.

These caveats were largely repeated in a wider study of schools councils by Taylor (2002). Secondary schools found more difficulties in initiating effective councils, partly from the nature of the schools themselves, and partly because of practical issues. There was a tendency to exclude younger pupils from participation, in both primary and secondary schools, and the focus of much discussion was on the improvement of school facilities (the playground, buildings and catering), on the organisation of the school day and on fundraising. There was little discussion of the curriculum and teaching styles, nor of issues such as consistency in school discipline, where inconsistencies in approach have been noted by Gillborn (1992) to be critical in developing racialised patterns of behaviour. Two-thirds of secondary teachers thought that councils are not worthwhile. More recent studies have indicated that schools councils that are carefully structured, with class or year-based meetings feeding into whole schools structures and reporting back may be both more popular and more effective (Whitty and Wisby, 2007; Davies and Yamashita, 2007).

Schools as institutions need to become infused with democratic processes: this is equally true of classrooms. The second set of features identified in Deacon Crick's analysis concern the introduction of dialogic processes into teaching and learning. Traditional models of teaching focus on the transmission process, where the knowledge accumulated by the teacher is transmitted to the learner, and this necessitates both a hierarchical power relationship, itself inimical to 'democratic' processes, and a denial of the identity and experience of the learner, whose previous understandings of and encounters with social life are overwritten by the teacher's narrative.

Introducing students' experience as valid data for learning requires a form of dialogue between pupils and teacher, and pupils and pupils, that acknowledges a partnership in exploring ideas. The traditional questioning style of teachers is often simply designed to elicit a repetition of the knowledge the teacher already possesses from the student (Galton *et al*, 1980; Delamont, 1986; Wragg and Brown, 2001). For example, if the teacher asks a class 'How many members of the legislature are there?' no one involved, teacher or pupils, actually imagines that this is a genuine question to which the teacher does not know the answer, and wants to find out how many legislators there are. Asking questions that are genuinely open-ended, to which the teacher doesn't already know the answer, and where the teacher accepts the response as supplying genuine fresh knowledge that will contribute to the development of the classroom discourse, is relatively uncommon, and can be as confusing for the student as it is a disconcerting role-shift for the teacher.

The content of what is discussed may in some ways make a transition to this form of discourse easier. Talking about identities – who do you feel you are, in this particular context – is an area in which it is evident to questioner and respondent alike that the terms of the reply are the property of the respondent. There's no possibility that the answer given will be either 'correct' or 'incorrect'. Osler and Starkey (2003) show how such conversations about multiple identities and loyalties can identify and extend conceptions of citizenship. The other suggested focus for the context of citizenship – the development of human rights – is equally an area in which divergences of views and opinions may be anticipated. Carter and Osler (2000) explore how human rights discussions were used to create positive interpersonal relationships and a culture consistent with human rights in classroom conversations with 14 and 15 year-old boys. They suggested that a fundamental development in classroom culture was needed to move from a collection of atomised individuals who lack the means to build relationships between members, towards the progressive establishment of democratic methods, so that students and staff have time to work with them. They reported that in the traditional classroom many students expressed the view that discussing human rights displayed weakness and need, and was not masculine. Rigid classroom approaches were antipathetic to the development of a school community, and rigid discipline reduced positive relationships.

Similar outcomes in secondary education were reported in a small-scale study of a theatre-in-education project by Day (2002). A focus on moral dilemmas allowed the students to move from particularistic data towards generalised principles. Building on students' own experiences of and familiarity with refugees and the homeless became possible because new interactive rules were introduced, different from the normal classroom approach: these allowed a new dialogic to emerge within which students participated as adults, and teachers as learners.

In primary schools, Holden (2000) described situations in which teachers had no policy for moral and social education, though they would describe these values as being paramount. But she observed that talk was used to develop moral and social development, and that children demonstrated a complex understanding of social relationships and morals from an early age. But citizenship education opportunities were missed by teachers, including opportunities of discussing rights and responsibilities beyond the school, democratic processes, rights and values, participation by pupils in debate and agenda setting (see also Claire and Holden, 2007). Clare *et al* (1996) show how teachers can develop conversational styles of discourse, particularly in identifying moral dilemmas in literature. They describe 9 year-old children initiating discussion of the values implicit in stories. However, this was not simply a consequence of reading the stories: the teacher had first to create situations of cognitive dissonance, focusing developmentally appropriate questions and helping pupils to work on them through interactive discussion. The teacher needed to be able to recognise appropriate dilemmas, and to present them within a facilitative pedagogy.

A dialogic classroom requires the development of a particular set of skills. Teachers need to manage discussions so that their students learn the skills of turn-taking, and of building on each others' experiences, points of view and arguments. Skills of decision making, and of accepting the consequences of one's decisions, can be initiated at a very young age, and then refined and differentiated over time. A wide series of procedural values and rules need to inform such a classroom: the need to listen to others as well as to articulate personal views, and to synthesise shared positions from these; the need to tolerate the substantive values of others; and a fundamental respect for truth and inquiry.

This remodelling of classroom interaction allows the valuing, understanding and acknowledgement of different experiences and points of view, and necessary to meet the requirements of citizenship. We might conclude by turning to a pioneer writer on education, Aristotle, on the meaning of being a good citizen:

> ... it is not possible to be a good ruler without first having been ruled. Not that good ruling and good obedience are the same virtue – only that the good citizen must have the knowledge and ability both to rule and be ruled. That is what we mean by the virtue of a citizen – understanding the governing of free men from both points of view. *The Politics*, Book III, Chapter iv (1277a33) (Sinclair, 1962)

Bibliography

Adams. R. (1972) *Watership Down*. Harmondsworth: Puffin

Ahier, J. and Ross, A. (eds) (1994) *The Social Subjects in the Curriculum*. London: Falmer

Almond, G. and Verba, S. (1963) *The Civic Culture: political attitudes and democracy in five nations*. Boston MA: Little, Brown

Anderson, B. (1983, 1991) *Imagined Communities: Reflections on the Origin and Spread of Nationalism* (revised ed). London: Verso

Appelt, H. and Irgang, W (1963) *Ruthenians: Schlesisches Urkundenbuch*. Gratz: Bohlau Verlag

Apple, M. (1990) *Ideology and Curriculum* (2nd edn). London: Routledge

Archer, L. (2003) *'Race' Masculinity and schooling: Muslim boys and education*. Buckingham: Open University Press

Aristotle, (1962) *The Politics* (trans Sinclair, T.). Harmondsworth: Penguin.

Arthur, W. (1994) Inductive Reasoning and Bounded Rationality. *American Economic Review*. 84 406-411

Ascherson, N. (1995) *Black Sea: the birthplace of civilisation and barbarism*. London: Cape

Audigier, F. (1998) *Basic Concepts and core competencies for education for democratic citizenship* (Project 'Education for Democratic Citizenship'). Strasbourg: Council for Cultural Co-operation DGIV/EDU/CIT (2000) 23

Avbelj, M. (2005) Can the New European Constitution Remedy the EU 'Democratic Deficit'?, *EUMAP On-line journal*, 2005/03/10 http://hdl.handle.net/1814/4166

Barth, F. (1969) *Ethnic Groups and Boundaries*. Oslo: Bergen

Bartlett, R. (1994) *The making of Europe: Conquest, Colonisation and Cultural Change 950-1350*. Harmondsworth: Penguin

Beck, U. (2008) Rights: Beyond methodological nationalism. *Re-public: re-imaging democracy*. [interview with Panos Papoulias] March 26th, 2008. at http://www.re-public.gr/en/?p =157

Beck, U. and Grande, E. (2007) *Cosmopolitan Europe*. Cambridge: Polity Press

Bell, A. and Sethares, W. (2001) Avoiding Global Congestion using Decentralized Adaptive Agents. *IEEE transactions on Signal Processing*, 49 2873-79

Benabou, R. and Tirole, J. (2005) Incentives and Prosocial Behaviour, *Working Paper No. 11535*, NBER Program. at http://www.nber.org/papers/w11535

Berger, P. and Luckman, T. (1966) *The Social Construction of Reality*. Harmondsworth: Penguin

Billig, M. (1995) *Banal Nationalism*. London: Sage

Blyth, W. A. L. (1967) *English Primary Education* (2 vols) London: Routledge and Kegan Paul

Borhaug, K. (1999) Education for Democracy. In Ross, A. (ed) *Young Citizens in Europe*. London: CiCe

Bottery, M. (2003) The End of Citizenship? The Nation State, Threats to its Legitimacy, and Citizenship Education in the Twenty-first Century. *Cambridge Journal of Education*, 33 1 1

Boud, D., Keogh, R. and Walker, D. (eds) (1985) *Reflection. Turning experience into learning.* London: Kogan Page

Boud, D., Cohen, R., Walker, D. (1993) *Using Experience for Learning.* Buckingham: Open University Press

Bourdieu, P (1971) Intellectual Field and Creative Project. in Young, M.F.D. (ed) *Knowledge and Control.* London: Collier-Macmillan

Bourdieu, P. (1974) The School as a Conservative Force: Scholastic and Cultural Inequalities [*L'École Conservatrice*, in *Revue française de sociologie*, 7 (1966) trans J. Whitehouse, in Eggleston, J. (ed) *Research in the Sociology of Education.* London: Methuen

Bowles, S. and Gintis, H. (1976) *Schooling in capitalist America: Educational reform and contradictions of economic life.* New York: Basic Books

Bowles, S. and Gintis, H. (1980) Contradiction and reproduction in educational theory. in. L. Barton, R. Meigham and S. Walker (Eds.), *Schooling, ideology, and the curriculum.* London: Falmer

Bowles, S. and Gintis, H. (1988) Schooling in Capitalist America: Reply to our critics. in Cole, M. (ed) *Bowles and Gintis Revisited: Correspondence and Contradiction in Educational Theory.* London: Falmer

Bowles, S. and Gintis, H. (2003) Prosocial emotions *Santa Fe Institute Working Papers* 02-07-028 http://www.santafe.edu/research/publications/workingpapers/02-07-028.pdf

Bromley, C., Curtice, J., and Seyd, B. (2004) *Is Britain Facing a Crisis of Democracy?* Centre for Research into Elections and Social Trends: Working paper. http://www.crest.ox.ac.uk/papers/p106.pdf

Brubaker, R. and Cooper, F. (2000) Beyond Identity, *Theory and Society*, 29 1 1-47

Bruner, J. (1966a) *Towards a Theory of Instruction.* Cambridge MA, Harvard University Press

Bruner, J. (1966b) On Education: An Exchange Between Jerome Bruner and John Holt, *New York Review of Books*, 6 8 (May 12, 1966) at http://www.nybooks.com/

Bruner, J. and Haste, H. (eds) (1987) *Making Sense: The Child's Construction of the World.* London: Methuen

Carraher, D.W. and Schliemann, A.D. (2000) Lessons from everyday reasoning in mathematics education: Realism versus meaningfulness. in Jonassen, D. and Land, S. (eds) *Theoretical Foundations of Learning Environments.* Mahwah, NJ, Lawrence Erlbaum

Carter, C. and Osler, A. (2000) Human Rights, Identities and Conflict Management: A study of school culture as experienced through classroom relationships. *Cambridge Journal of Education*, 30 3 335-356

Claire, H. (2001) *Not Aliens: primary school children and the Citizenship/PSHE curriculum.* Stoke on Trent: Trentham Books

Claire, H. and Holden, C. (eds) (2007) *The Challenge of Teaching Controversial Issues.* Stoke on Trent: Trentham

Clare, L., Gallimore, R. and Patthey-Chavez, G. (1996) Using Moral Dilemmas in Children's Literature as a vehicle for moral education and teaching reading comprehension, *Journal of Moral Education.* 25 3 325-341

Clarke, S. (2007) The Trajectory of 'Political Education" in English Schools: The Rise and Fall of Two Initiatives, *Citizenship, Teaching and Learning*, 3 1 3-16

Cleaver, E. and Nelson, J. (2006) Active citizenship: from policy to practice, *Education Journal*, 98 34-37

Coase, R. (1988) *The Firm, the Market and the Law.* Chicago IL: University of Chicago Press

Cohen, A. (1994) *Self Consciousness: An Alternative Anthropology of Identity.* London: Routledge

Cohen, A. (1998) Boundaries and Boundary-Consciousness: Politicising Cultural Identity, in Anderson, M.,and Bort, E. (eds) *The Frontiers of Europe.* London: Printer Press

Coles, M. (1988) *Bowles and Gintis revisited: correspondence and contradiction in educational theory.* London: Falmer

Coles, R. (1986) *The Political Life of Children.* Boston MA: Houghton Mifflin

Colley, L. (1992) *Britons: Forging the Nation 1701 to 1837.* New Haven AM: Yale University Press

Connell, R. (1971) *The Child's Construction of Politics.* Calton: Melbourne University Press

Council of Europe (1950) *The European Convention on Human Rights* [adopted Rome, 4 November 1950]. Strasbourg: Council of Europe

Council of Europe (2002) *What is Education for Democratic Citizenship – Concepts and Practice.* at http://www.coe.int

Crick, B. (1974) Basic Political Concepts and Curriculum Development. *Teaching Politics*, 3, 1

Crick, B. (1998) *Education for Citizenship and the Teaching of Democracy in Schools* [Report of the Advisory Group on Education for Citizenship]. London: Qualifications and Curriculum Authority

Crick, B, and Lister, I. (1979) Political Literacy: The Centrality of the Concept. *International Journal of Political Education*, 1 1 1-12

Crick, B. and Porter, A. (1978) *Political education and political literacy.* London: Longman for the Hansard Society

Criddle, E., Vidovich, L. and O'Neill, M. (2004) Discovering democracy: an analysis of curriculum policy for citizenship education, *Westminster Studies in Education*, 27 1 27-41

Cullen, J., Batterbury, S., Foresti, M. Lyons, C. and Stern, E. (1999) *Informal Learning and Widening Participation.* London: Department for Education and Enterprise

Dale, R., Esland, G., and Macdonald, M. (eds) (1976) *Schooling and Capitalism: A sociological reader.* London: Routledge and Kegan Paul/Open University Press

Davies, I. (1994) Whatever Happened to Political Education? *Educational Review,* 46 2 15-27

Davies, I. (1999) What has Happened to the Teaching of Politics in Schools in England During the Last Three Decades and Why? *Oxford Review of Education*, 25 1 2 125-140

Davies, I., Evans, M. and Reid, A. (2005) Globalising Citizenship Education? A Critique of'Global Education' and'Citizenship Education', *British Journal of Educational Studies*, 53 1 66-89

Davies, I. and Issitt, J. (2005) Reflections on citizenship education in Australia, Canada and England, *Comparative Education*, 41 4 389-410

Davies, L. (2006) Global citizenship: abstraction or framework for action?, *Educational Review*, 58 1 5-25

Davies, L. and Yamashita, H. (2007) *Schools Councils – School Improvements: The London Secondary School Councils Action Research Project.* London: Schools Council UK/ Birmingham: Centre for International Education and Research

Davies, N. (1996) *Europe: A History.* Oxford: Oxford University Press

Day, L. (2002) 'Putting yourself in other people's shoes': The use of Forum Theatre to explore refugee and homeless issues in school. *Journal of Moral Education*, 31 1 21-34

145

Deakin Crick, R. (2002) *Transforming Visions, Managing Values in Schools: A Case Study.* Bristol: Middlesex University Press

Deakin Crick, R., Coates, M., Taylor, M. and Ritchie, S. (2004) *A Systematic Review of the Impact of Citizenship Education on the Provision of Schooling.* London: EPPI-Centre

Delamont, S. (1986) *Inside the Secondary Classroom.* London: Routledge and Kegan Paul

Denscombe, M. and Conway, L. (1982) Autonomy and Control in Curriculum Innovation: A Case study of Development Education in the Primary School. *Teaching Politics,* 11, 3

Dewey, J. (1907) *The School and Society.* Chicago IL: University of Chicago Press

Dewey, J. (1929) *Experience and Nature.* New York NY: Dover

Dewey, J. (1933) *How We Think. A restatement of the relation of reflective thinking to the educative process* (rev edn). Boston MA: D. C. Heath.

Durkheim, E (1956) *Education and Sociology.* New York NY: The Free Press

Durkheim, E. (1897) (1970) *The Suicide: A study in sociology.* London: Routledge and Kegan Paul

Easton D, and Dennis, J. (1969) *Children in the Political System.* New York NY: McGraw Hill

Electoral Commission (2005) Election 2005 Turnout: How Many, *Who and Why?* at http://www.electoralcommission.org.uk/files/dms/Election2005turnoutFINAL_18826-13874__E__N__S__W__.pdf

Electoral Commission (2008) *Interactive Results Service: UK Parliamentary general election, May 2005 results and European Parliamentary election, 10 June 2004 (results for the UK).* at hhttp://www.electoralcommission.org.uk/election-data/index.cfm

Euractive (2004) *European Parliament Elections 2004: results* (30 June 2004.) at http://www.euractiv.com/en/elections/european-parliament-elections-2004-results/article-117482

European Commission (1997) *Towards a Europe of Knowledge*: Communication from the commission 97(563). Brussels: European Commission

European Opinion Research Group (2004) *Joint Full Report of Eurobarometer 61 and Eurobarometer 2004.1* (EB61) Brussels: European Commission. at http://ec.europa.eu/public_opinion/archives/eb/eb61/eb61_en.pdf

European Union (1992) *Treaty on European Union*, Maastricht. *Official Journal* C 191, 29 July 1992

European Union (1993) *Green Paper on the European Dimension in Education*, 29 September 1993. COM (93) 457 final, 29 September 1993

European Union (2000a) *Charter of Fundamental Rights of the European Union*. Nice: European Union

European Union (2000b) *Lisbon European Council, 23 and 24 March 2000, Presidency Conclusions*. Lisbon; European Union

Fass, D. (2007) Turkish youth in the European knowledge economy: An exploration of their responses to Europe and the role of social class and school dynamics for their identities. *European Societies* 9 4 573-599

Fass, D. (2008) Reconsidering Identity: The ethnic and political dimensions of hybridity among majority and Turkish youth in Germany and England. Paper presented at the 10th CiCe conference, Istanbul, May 2008.

Fehr, E. and Gachter, S. (2000b) Fairness and Retaliation: The economics of recipriocity, *Economic Perspectives* 14 19-81

Fehr, E. and Gachter, S. (2000a) Cooperation and punishment in public good experiments *American Economic Review.* 90 980-94

Fischer, J (2000) *From Confederacy to Federation: Thoughts on the Finality of European Integration.* Speech at the Humboldt University in Berlin, 12 May 2000, at www.jeanmonnet program.org/papers/00/joschka_fischer_en.rtf

Flecknoe, M. (2002) Democracy, Citizenship and School Improvement: What can one school tell us?, *School Leadership and Management.* 22 4 421-437

Foucault, M. (1978) *The History of Sexuality, Volume 1: An introduction.* Harmondsworth, Penguin

Fügedi, E (1975) *Das mittelalterlicke Konigreich Ungarn als Galtland,* in Schleisinger, W (ed) *Die deutsche Ostseiddlung als Problem der europeischen Geschichte.* Thorbecke: Sigmaringen

Galton, M., Simon, B. and Croll, P. (1980) *Inside the Primary Classroom.* London: Routledge and Kegan Paul

Gear, J., McIntosh, A. and Squires, G. (1994) *Informal learning in the professions.* Hull: University of Hull

Geertz, C. (ed.) (1972) *Myth, Symbol and Culture.* New York NY: Norton

Geertz, C. (1973) *The Interpretation of Culture.* New York NY: Basic Books

Gellner, E. (1983) *Nations and Nationalism.* Oxford: Basil Blackwell

Gergen, K (1994) *Realities and Relationships: Sounding in Social Construction.* Cambridge, MA: Harvard University Press

Gibbon, E. (1994/1776) *The History of the Decline and Fall of the Roman Empire* (ed Womersley, D). London: Allen Lane

Giddens, A. (1984) *The Constitution of Society.* Cambridge: Polity Press

Giddens, A. (1991) *Modernity and Self-Identity: Self and Society in the Late Modern Age.* Cambridge: Polity

Gillborn, D. (1992) Citizenship, 'race' and the Hidden Curriculum, *International Studies in the Sociology of Education,* 2 1 57-73

Gintis, H., Bowles, S., Boyd, R. and Fehr, E. (2003) Explaining altruistic behaviour in humans. *Evolution and Human Behavior* 24 153-172

Goffman, E. (1969) *Presentation of the self in everyday life.* London: Alan Lane

Golby, M. (1989) Curriculum Tradition. in Moon, B., Murphy, P. and Raynor, J. (eds) *Policies for the Curriculum.* London: Hodder and Stoughton

Goodson, I. (1987) *School Subjects and Curriculum Change: Studies in Curriculum History* (revised edn). London: Falmer

Gramsci (1971) *Selections from the Prison Notebooks*, trans Hoare, Q. and Nowell Smith, G. London: Lawrence and Wishart

Green, A. (1990) *Education and State Formation: The rise of Education systems in England, France and the USA.* London: Macmillan

Greenstein, F. (1965) *Children and Politics.* Harvard MA:Yale University Press

Gundara J. (2006) The Sacred and the Secular: Multiple Citizenship and Education, in Sprogøe, J. and Winther-Jensen, T. (eds) *Identity, Education and Citizenship and Multiple Interrelations.* Frankfurt am Main: Peter Lang

Haar, J. Nielsen, T., Hansen, M., Jakobsen, S. (2005) *Explaining Student Performance: Evidence from the International PISA, TIMSS and PIRLS surveys.* Kobenhaven: Danish Technological Institute

Habermas, J. (1976) *Zur Rekonstrutktion des historischen Materialismus.* Frankfurt: Suhrkamp

147

Hagstrom, W. (1982) Gift giving as an organizing principle in science. in Barnes, B. and Edge, D. (eds) *Science in Context: Readings in the Sociology of Science*. Cambridge, MA: MIT Press.

Hall, E. (1989) *Inventing the Barbarian*. Oxford: Oxford University Press

Hall, S. (1992) New Ethnicities. in Rattansi, A. and Donald, J. (eds) *Race, Culture and Difference*. London: Sage

Hall, S. (1996) Introduction: Who needs identity? in Hall, S. and du Gay, P. (eds) *Questions of Cultural Identity*. London: Sage

Hall, S. (1997) Representation, Meaning and Language: The Spectacle of the 'Other'. in Hall, S. (ed) *Representation: Cultural Representations and Signifying Practices*. London: Sage

Hammerstein (2003) Why is reciprocity so rare in animals? A protestant appeal. in Hammerstein, P. (ed) *Genetic and Cultural Evolution of Cooperation*. Cambridge MA: MIT Press, pp 83-94

Harbaugh, W., Krause, K. and Liday, S. (2002) *Children's Bargaining Behaviour: Working Paper*. Albuquerque NM: University of New Mexico. http://harbaugh.uoregon.edu/Children/index.htm

Heater, D. (1990) *Citizenship*. London: Longmans

Heater, D. and Oliver, D. (1994) *The Foundations of Citizenship*. Hemel Hempstead: Harvester Wheatsheaf

Hegel. G. (2007) The Greek World, in *The Philosophy of History*. Cosimo, Inc

Held, D. (1991) Democracy, the Nation-State and the Global System, in D. Held (ed) *Political Theory Today,* pp. 227-35. Cambridge: Polity Press

Held, D. (1995) *Democracy and the Global Order. From the Modern State to Cosmopolitan Governance*. Cambridge: Polity Press

Henrich, J., Boyd, R., Bowles, S., Camerer, C., Fehr, E., Gintis, H., McElreath, R. Alvard, M., Barr, A., Ensminger, J., Hill, K., Gil-White, F., Gurven, M., Marlowe, F., Patton, J., Smith, N. and Tracer, D. (forthcoming) 'Economic Man' in Cross-cultural Perspective: Behavioural Experiments in 15 Small-scale Societies. *Behavioural and Brain Science* at http://www.bbsonline.org/Preprints/Henrich/Referees/

Herder, J. (2002) *Ideas for the Philosophy of History of Humanity* (1784-91) *Philosophical Works,* (ed Forster. M.). Cambridge: Cambridge University Press

Herodotus (1972) *The Histories* (trans and ed de Selincourt, A.). Harmondsworth: Penguin

Herrin, J. (2007) *Byzantium: The Surprising Life of a Medieval Empire*. London: Allen Lane

Hess, R. and Torney, J. (1967) *The Development of Political Attitudes in Children*. Chicago IL: Aldine

Hey, V. (1997) *The Company She Keeps: An ethnography of girls' friendship*. Buckingham: Open University Press

Hirschhorn, J. (2006) *Delusional Democracy: Fixing the Republic Without Overthrowing the Government*. Monroe, ME: Common Courage Press

Hladnik, M. (1995) All Different – All Equal: who defines ediucation for citizenship in a new Europe?' in Osler, A, Rathenow, H-F and Starkey, H., (eds) *Teaching for Citizenship in Education*. Stoke on Trent: Trentham

Hobbes, T. (1651) *The Leviathan, or the Matter, Forme & Power of a Common-wealth, Ecclesiasticall and Civill.* London: Andrew Crooke at the Green Dragon

Hobsbawm, E. and Ranger, T. (eds) (1983) *The Invention of Tradition*.Cambridge: Cambridge University Press

Hodges, R. and Whitehouse, D. (1983) *Mohammed, Charlemagne and the Origins of Europe: Archaeology and the Pirenne Thesis*. New York NY: Cornell University Press

Holden, C. (2000) Ready for Citizenship? A case study of approaches to social and moral education in two contrasting primary schools in the UK', *The School Field: International Journal of Theory and Research in Education*, 11 1 117-130

Holden C (2006) Concerned citizens: children and the future, *Education, Citizenship and Social Justice*, 1, 3, 231-247

Hutchings, M, Fulop, M., and Van den Dries, A-M. (eds) (2002) *Young People's Understanding of Economic Issues in Europe*. Stoke on Trent: Trentham

ILEA [Inner London Education Authority] (1980) *Social Studies in the Primary School (ILEA Curriculum Guidelines)*. London: ILEA Learning Materials Service

Ireland, E., Kerr, F., Lopes, J. and Nelson, J. (2006) *Active Citizenship and Young people: Opportunities, Experiences and Challenges in and beyond School. Citizenship Education Longitudinal Study: Fourth Annual report*. London: Department for Education and Skills

Isaacs, K. (ed) (2008) *Images of Europe: From within and beyond*. Pisa: Pisa University Press

Jamieson, L. (2002) Theorising Identity, Nationality and Citizenship: Implications for European Citizenship Identity. *Sociológia*, 34 6 507-532

Jamieson, L. (2005) SERD-2000-00260 *Final report: Orientations of Young Men and Women to Citizenship and European Identity*. http://www.socresonline.org.uk/10/3/grundy.html

Jardine, L. (1999) *Ingenious Pursuits: Building the Scientific Revolution*. London: Little, Brown

Jarvis, P. (1987) *Adult Learning in the Social Context*. London: Croom Helm

Jarvis, P. (1995) *Adult and Continuing Education. Theory and practice* (2nd ed), London: Routledge

Jenkins, R. (1996) *Social Identity*. London: Routledge

Jencks, C (1972) *Inequality: A reassessment of the effects of family and schooling in America*. New York: Basic Books

Jensen, M. C. (2001a) Corporate budgeting is broken – let's fix it, *Harvard Business Review* November, 94 -101

Jensen, M. C. (2001b) Paying People to Lie: the truth about the Budgeting Process. *Harvard Business School working paper 01-072*. at http://papers.ssrn.com/papers=267651

Jones, J. (2005) The Evil Empire. *The Guardian* (London). 8 September 2005

Judt, T. (2006) *Postwar: a History of Europe since 1945*. London: Penguin

Kelty, C. (2001) Free Software, Free Science *First Monday* 6, 12 http://www.firstmonday.org/issues/issue6_12/kelty/

Kenendy, J. K. (2006) Towards a conceptual framework for understanding Active and passive Citizenship. Unpublished, quoted in Nelson, J. and Kerr, D., 2006.

Kerr, D. and Ireland, E. (2004) Making Citizenship Education Real, *Education Journal.* 78, 25-27

Kidder, R. (2002) The strength to care, *Times Educational Supplement,* Scotland. 12 April 2002 21

Kinder, D. and Kiewiet, D. (1979) Economic discontent and political behaviour: the role of personal grievances ad collective economic judgements in Congressional voting. *American Journal of Political Science.* 79, 10-27

Kinder, D. and Kiewiet, D. (1981) Sociotropic Politics: The American Case. *British Journal of Politics.* 11 129-61

Kirsch, I., Long, J. D., Lafontaine, D., McQueen, J., *et al.* (2002). *Reading for Change: performance and engagement across countries*. Paris, OECD

Knack, S. and Keefer, P. (2001) Trust, Associational Life and Economic Performance in Helliwell Hull, J. (ed) *The Contribution of Human and Social Capital to Sustained Economic Growth and Well being*. Château Frontenac, Québec Canada: Human Resources Development/ OECD 181

Kolb, D. A. (1976) *The Learning Style Inventory: Technical Manual*. Boston, MA: McBer

Kolb, D. A. (1984) *Experiential Learning*. Englewood Cliffs, NJ: Prentice Hall.

Kolb. D. A. and Fry, R. (1975) 'Toward an applied theory of experiential learning, in C. Cooper (ed) *Theories of Group Process*. London: John Wiley.

Kowabura, K. (2000) Linux; a bazaar at the edge of chaos. *First Monday* 5 http://firstmonday. org/issues/issue5-3/kuwabara/index.html

Lave, J. and Chaiklin, S. (eds.) (1993) *Understanding Practice: Perspectives on Activity and Context*. Cambridge: University of Cambridge Press

Lave, J. and E. Wenger, E, (1991) *Situated learning: Legitimate peripheral participation*. Cambridge: Cambridge University Press

Lawton, D. (1975) *Class, Culture and the Curriculum*. London: Routledge and Kegan Paul

Lawton, D. and Gordon, P (1996) *Dictionary of Education* (2nd edn). London: Hodder and Stoughton

Le Goff, J. (2005) *The Birth of Europe: 400 to 1500*. Oxford: Blackwell

Leighton, R. (2004) The nature of citizenship education provision: an initial study, *Curriculum Journal*. 15 2 167-181

Levi, M. (1999) State of Trust. in V Braithwaite and M Levi (eds) *Trust and Governance*. New York: Russell Sage Foundation

Locke, J. (1690) *Two Treatises on Government*. London: Millar, Woodfall

Lomax, D (1978) *The Reconquest of Spain*. London: Longman

Lutz, W., Kritzinger, S. and Skirbekk, V. (2006) The Demography of Growing European Identity, *Science*, 314 5798 425

Lyotard, J-F, (1984) *The postmodern condition: A report on knowledge*. Minneapolis MN: University of Minnesota Press

Mac an Ghaill, M. (1994) *The Making of Men: Masculinities, Sexualities and Schooling*. Buckingham: Open University Press

Mackenzie, W. J. M. (1978) *Political Identity*. Harmondsworth: Penguin

Mannitz, S. (2004a) Pupils' Negotiations of Cultural Difference: Identity Management and Discursive Assimilation. in Schiffauer, W., Baumann, G., Kastoryano, R, and . Vertyovec, D. (eds) *Civic Enculturation: Nation-State, School and Ethnic Difference in the Netherlands, Britain, Germany and France*. New York: Berghahn Books

Mannitz, S. (2004b) Limitation, Convergence and Crossovers. in Schiffauer, W., Baumann, G., Kastoryano, R, and . Vertyovec, D. (eds) *Civic Enculturation: Nation-State, School and Ethnic Difference in the Netherlands, Britain, Germany and France*. New York: Berghahn Books

Margerison, C. (1968) Island: A social studies experiment, *Ideas*, 8/9, Goldsmith College Curriculum Laboratory

Margerison, C., (1972) A learning experiment in social studies education: aspects of children's political understanding and development, *Teaching Politics*, 1 1

Marshall, T. H. (1950) *Citizenship and social class and other essays*. Cambridge: Cambridge University Press

Maylor, U., Read, B., Mendick, H., Ross, A. and Rollock, N. (2007) *Diversity and Citizenship in the Curriculum: Research Review* [Research Report RR 819]. London: Department for Education and Skills

McGettrick, B. (2002) *Emerging Conceptions of Scholarship, Service and Teaching*. Toronto: Canadian Society for the Study of Education

Merton, R. (1988) The Matthew Effect in Science: 2 – Cumulative Advantage and the Symbolism of Intellectual Property, *ISIS* 79 607-623

Michalowski, P. (2006) The Cyrus Cylinder, in *Historical Sources in Translation*. Oxford: Blackwell

Mill, J. S. (1967/2005) *Dissertations and Discussions, Political, Philosophical, and Historical*. London: Longmans Green/London: Elibron Classics

Millor, W. Butler, H. and Brooke, C. (eds) (1986) *John of Salisbury: The Early Letters (1153-61)*. Oxford: Clarendon Press

Mirabeau, H. (1782) *Des Lettres de Cachet et des prisons d'état*. Hamburg: Halblederband der Zeit

Mitchell, J. (2005) The European Union's "Democratic Deficit": Bridging the Gap between Citizens and EU Institutions, *EUMAP On-line journal*, 2005/03/10. www.eumap.org/journal/features/2005/demodef/mitchell/.

Mittone, L. (2003) Altruism without reciprocation in children. *Computable and Experimental Economics Laboratory Working Paper 0302*, Trento: Department of Economics, University of Trento. http://ideas.repec.org/s/trn/utwpce.html

Modood, T. and Werbner P. (Eds.) (1997). *The Politics of Multiculturalism in the New Europe: Racism, Identity and Community*. London: Zed Books

Mokyr, J. (2002) *The Gift of Athena: Historical Origins of the Knowledge Economy*. Princeton: Princeton University Press

Monnet, J. (1976) *Memoirs*. London: Collins

Montaigne, M. (1965) Of Cannibals, in *The Complete Essays of Michel de Montaigne*, ed D M Frame. Palo Alto CA: Stanford University Press

Montero, C. (1992) The concept of citizenship in the treaty on European Union, *Common Market Law Review*, 29, 1139

Moravsci, K. A. (2004) Is there a democratic deficit in world politics? A framework for Analysis, *Government and Opposition*, 39 2 336-363

Moreno L. (1997) *La Federalización de España: Poder Político y Territorio*. Madrid: Siglo Veintiuno de España

Murnigham, J. and Saxon, M. (1998) Ultimatum Bargaining by Children and Adults. *Journal of Economic Psychology*. 19 415-445

Murphy, P. (ed) (1999) *Learners, Learning and Assessment*. London: Paul Chapman

Murray, O. (1970) The Ionian Revolt, in *Cambridge Ancient History Volume IV: Persia, Greece and the Eastern Mediterranean*. Cambridge: Cambridge University Press

Nelson, J. and Kerr, D. (2006) *Active Citizenship in INCA countries: definitions, policies, practices and outcomes: Final Report*. London: Qualification and Curriculum Authority

Oakeshott, M. J.(1933) *Experience and its modes*. Cambridge: Cambridge University Press

OECD (2001) *Knowledge and Skills for Life: First results of the OECD programme for International Student Assessment (PISA)* 2000, Paris: OECD

Orwell, G. (1945) *Animal Farm*. London: Secker and Warburg

Osler, A. and Starkey, H. (2003) Learning for Cosmopolitan Citizenship: theoretical debates and young people's experiences, *Educational Review.* 55 3 243-255

Pirenne, H. (1936) *Mohammed and Charlemagne.* New York NY: Dover

Popper, K. (1959) *The Logic of Scientific Discovery.* London: Routledge

Preuss, U. K. (1996) Two Challenges to European Citizenship. in Bellamy, R and Castiglione, D. (eds) *Constitutionalism in Transformation: European and Theoretical Perspectives.* Oxford: Blackwell

Prior, W. (2006) Civics and citizenship education, *Ethos,* 14 3 6-7

Ramsden, P. (1992) *Learning to Teach in Higher Education.* London: Routledge

Rawls, J. (1971) *A Theory of Justice.* Oxford: Oxford University Press

Renan, E. (1882) *What is a Nation? (Qu'est-ce qu'une nation?),* Lecture given at the Sorbonne, 11 March 1882, in Discours et Conferences, Paris, Calman-Levy, 1887, pp.277-310; also in Eley, G. and Suny, G. (eds) (1996) *Becoming National: A Reader.* Oxford: Oxford University Press

Rex, J. (1996a) National Identity in the Democratic Multi-Cultural State, *Sociological Research Online,* 1 (2) http://www.socresonline.org.uk/socresonline/1/2/1.html.

Rex, J. (1996b) Contemporary Nationalism, Its Causes and Consequences for Europe – A Reply to Delanty, *Sociological Research Online,* 1 (4) http://www.socresonline.org.uk/socresonline/1/4/rex.html

Riches, J. (1974) Education for Democracy: A curriculum unit for Upper Juniors. *Teaching Politics,* 3 2 (and second part, 3 3)

Rifkin, J. (2004) *The European Dream: How Europe's Vision of the Future Is Quietly Eclipsing the American Dream.* New York: Tarcher

Robbins, D. (1990) *The Work of Pierre Bourdieu: Recognising Society.* Buckingham: Open University Press

Robbins, M., Francis, L. and Elliott, E. (2003) Attitudes toward education for global citizenship among trainee teachers, *Research in Education,* 69 93-98

Robins, L. and Robins, V. (1978) Politics in the First Year: this year, next year, sometime... never. *Teaching Politics,* 7 1

Rogoff, B. (1990) *Apprenticeship in Thinking.* New York NY: Oxford University Press

Rogoff, B. (2003). *The cultural nature of human development.* New York NY: Oxford University Press

Rogoff, B., Goodman Turkanis, C., and Bartlett, L. (2001) *Learning together: Children and adults in a school community.* New York NY: Oxford University Press

Ross, A. (1981) Using literature to develop political concepts in the primary school. *Teaching Politics,* 10 1

Ross, A. (2000) *Curriculum: Construction and Critique.* London: Falmer

Ross, A (2004) Erasmus and the Experience of Citizenship, in Ross A (ed) *The Experience of Citizenship.* London: CiCe

Ross, A. (2008) The Image of Europe: The social dimension. in Isaacs, K. (ed) *Images of Europe: From within and beyond.* Pisa: Pisa University Press

Ross, A., Fülöp, M. and Kuščer, N. (2006) *Teachers' and Pupils' Constructions of Competition and Cooperation: A three-country study of Slovenia, Hungary and England.* University of Ljubljana: Ljubljana

Roth, A. and Prasniker, V. (1991) Bargaining and Market Behaviour in Jerusalem, Ljublijana, Pittsburgh and Tokyo: An Experimental Study. *American Economic Review.* 81 1068-95

Roy, D. (1952) Quota Restrictions and Goldbricking in a Machine Shop. *American Journal of Sociology* 7 427-42

Russell, J. (2002) Moral Consciousness in a Community of Inquiry. *Journal of Moral Education.* 31 2 142-153

Rutter, M., Maughn, B., Mortimore, P. and Outson, J. (1979) *Fifteen Thousand Hours: secondary schools and their effects on children.* London: Open Books

Ryle, G. (1949) *The Concept of Mind.* Chicago: The University of Chicago Press

Said, E. (1978) *Orientalism.* New York: Vintage

Säljö, R. (1979) Learning in the learner's perspective. I. Some common-sense conceptions, *Reports from the Institute of Education, University of Gothenburg,* 76

Sangrador, G. J. L. (1996) *Identidades, actitudes y estereotipos en la España de las autonomìas.* Madrid, Spain: Centro de Investigaciones Sociales

Sassoon, D. (2006) *The Culture of the Europeans.* London: Harper Collins

Schissler, H. and Sosyal, Y. (2004) *The Nation, Europe and the World: Textbooks and Curricula in Transition.* New York: Berghahn Books

Schultze, W. (2004) *Mutatio-Innovatio – Zugänge zur Wahrnehmung von Veränderung in der Frühen Neuzeit,* ms,Munich, cited in Beck U and Grande E (2007) *Cosmopolitan Europe.* Cambridge: Polity

Sears, D. and Funk, C. (1990) Self-Interest in American's Political Opinions. in Mansbridge, J. (ed) *Beyond Self Interest.* Chicago: University of Chicago Press

Selbourne, D. (1994) *The Principle of Duty,* London: Sinclair Stevenson

Sen, A. (2006) *Identity and Violence: The Illusion of Destiny.* London: Allen Lane

Senesh, L. (1968) The pattern of the economic curriculum, *Social Education,* 32 Jan 1968 47-50

Sheehan, J. (2008) *Where Have All the Soldiers Gone? The Transformation of Modern Europe.* New York: Houghton Mifflin

Shore, C. and Black, A. (1994) Citizen's Europe and the Construction of European Identity. in Goddard, V., Llobera, J. and Shore, C. (eds) *The Anthropology of Europe.* Oxford: Berg

Shotter, J. and Gergen, K. (eds) (1990) *Texts of Identity.* London: Sage

Sinclair, T. (ed) (1962) *Aristotle: The Politics.* Harmondsworth: Penguin

Sliwka, A. (2006) Controversial Issues in German Secondary Schools: The deliberation project, paper presented at the Second International CitizED conference, Oxford, July 2006. at http://www.citized.info/pdf/ejournal/conf_2006/013.pdf

Smith, A. (1776/1973) *An Inquiry into the Nature and Causes of the Wealth of Nations.* Canaan edition in the Modern Library Series. New York NY: Random House

Smith, A. (1991) *National Identity.* Harmondsworth: Penguin

Smith, A. (1995) *Nations and Nationalism in a Global Era.* Cambridge: Polity Press

Smith, A.D. (1986) *The Ethnic Origin of Nations.* Oxford: Blackwell

Smith, V. (2003) Constructivist and Ecological Rationality in Economics. *American Economic Review* 93 465-508

Solana, J (1998) Securing peace in Europe, Speech at the *NATO Symposium on the political relevance of the 1648 Peace of Westphalia,* Munster 12 Nov 1998, at http://www.nato.int/docu/speech/1998/s981112a.htm

Solla Price D. de and Beaver, D. (1966) Collaboration in an Invisible College. *American Psychologist.* 21 1101-17

Soysal, Y. (1997) Changing Citizenship in Europe: Remarks on Postnational Membership and the Nation State. in Cesarini, D. and M. Fulbook, M. (eds) *Citizenship, Nationality and Migration in Europe*. London: Routledge

Soysal, Y. (2002) *Rethinking Nation State Identities in the New Europe: A cross-national study of school curricula and textbooks*. ESRC End of Grant Report L213252018 Wivenhoe: University of Essex

Soysal, Y. (2006) How Europe Teaches Itself? in Spogøe, J. and Winther-Jensen, T. (eds) *Identity, Education and Citizenship and Multiple Interrelations*. Frankfurt am Main: Peter Lang

Steenbergen, B. van (1994) Towards a Global Ecological Condition of Citizenship in B. van Stenbergen (ed) *The Condition of Citizenship*. London: Sage

Steiner, M. (1992) *World Studies 8-13: evaluating active learning*. Manchester: Manchester Metropolitan University, World Studies Trust

Steiner, M. (ed) (1996) *Developing the Global Teacher: theory and practice in initial teacher education*. Stoke on Trent: Trentham

Stephan, P. (1996) The Economics of Science. *Journal of Economic Literature* 34 1220-31

Stevens, O. (1982) *Children Talking Politics: Political Learning in Childhood*. Oxford: Martin Robertson

Surowiecki, J. (2004) *The Wisdom of Crowds*. New York: Anchor Books

Sutherland, M. (2002) Educating Citizens in Europe. *European Education*, 34 3 77

Sutter, M. (2005) *On the nature of fair behaviour and its development with age*. Max Plank Institute for Economics, Discussion Paper, Strategic Interaction Group http://ideas.repec.org/s/esi/discus.html

Tajfel, H. (ed) (1978) *Differentiations between Social Groups: Studies in Social Psychology*. London: Academic Press

Tajfel, H., and Turner, J. C. (1979) An integrative theory of intergroup conflict. in Austin, W. G. and Worchel, S. (eds), *The social psychology of intergroup relations*. 94-109. Monterey, CA: Brooks-Cole

Taylor, M. (2002) *Schools Councils: Their Role in Citizenship and Personal and Social Education*. Slough: National Foundation for Educational Research

Tennant, M. (1988, 1997) *Psychology and Adult Learning*. London: Routledge

Tilly, R. (1983) Moral Standards and Business Behaviour in Nineteenth Century Germany and Britain. in Kocka. J. and Mitchell, A. (ed) *Bourgeois Society in Nineteenth Century Europe*. Oxford: Berg

Titmuss, R. (1971) *The Gift Relationship: From Human Blood to Social Policy*. New York: Pantheon

Tizard, B. and Hughes, M. (1984) *Young Children Learning*. London: Fontana

Torvalds, L (2001) *Just for Fun*. New York: Harper

Traynor, I. (2007) Feminist, socialist, devout Muslim: woman who has thrown Denmark into turmoil, *The Guardian*, 16 May 2007

Turner, J. C. (1984) Social Identification and Psychological Group Formation. in Tajfel, H. (ed) *The Social Dimension: European developments in Social Psychology* Vol 2. Cambridge: Cambridge University Press

United Nations (1948) *The Universal Declaration of Human Rights* (adopted by the General Assembly of the United Nations on December 10 1948). New York: United Nations

United Nations (1966) *International Covenant on Economic, Social and Cultural Rights* (adopted by the General Assembly of the United Nations on 16 December 1966). New York: United Nations

United States (1776) *The Constitution of the United States*, Article 1

Urry, J. (1995) *Consuming Places*. London: Routledge

Urry, J. (1999) Globalisation and Citizenship. *Journal of World-Systems Research*, 5 2 311-324

Urry, J. (2000) *Sociology beyond Societies*. London: Routledge

Vasak, K. (1979/1982) For the Third Generation of Human Rights: The Rights of Solidarity (International Institute of Human Rights, Strasbourg, July 1979), cited in Alston, P., A Third Generation of Solidarity Rights: Progressive Development or Obfuscation of International Human Rights Law? (1982) *Netherlands International Law Review*, 29 307

Vellacott, P. (1961) *Prometheus Bound and Other Plays: Prometheus Bound, The Supplicant, Seven Against Thebes, The Persians*. Harmondsworth: Penguin

Verdun, A. (1998) The Institutional Design of EMU: A Democratic Deficit?, *Journal of Public Policy*, 18 107-132

Wagstaff, S. (1978) *Teacher's Guide: People Around Us – 1: Families*. London: Inner London Education Authority

Weber, E. (1976) *Peasants into Frenchmen: The Modernisation of Rural France 1870 – 1914*. Stanford CA: Stanford University Press

Wenger, E. (1998) *Communities of practice: Learning, meaning, and identity*. Cambridge: Cambridge University Press

Wenger, E. (1999) Communities of Practice. Learning as a social system, *Systems Thinker*, 9 5 1-10

Wenger, E. (2002) Today's complex problem solving requires multiple perspectives. in Wenger, E., McDermott, R., Snyder, W. (eds) *Cultivating Communities of Practice*. Boston MA: Harvard University Press

Widdicombe, S. and Woofitt. R. (1995) *The Language of Youth Subcultures: Social Identity in Action*. Hemel Hempstead: Harvester

Williams, R. (1961) *The Long Revolution*. London: Chatto and Windus

Whitty, G. and Wisby, E. (2007) *Real Decision Making? Schools Councils in Action*. [Research Report RR001]. London: Department for Children Schools and Families

Wragg E. and Brown, G. (2001) *Questioning in the secondary school*. London: RoutledgeFalmer

Zalta, E. (ed) (2007) *Stanford Encyclopedia of Philosophy*. Stanford, CA: Stanford University Centre for the Study of Language and Information . at http://plato.stanford.edu/

Zuckerman, H. (1967) Nobel Laureates in Science: patterns of productive Collaboration and Authorship. *American Sociological Review* 32 391-403

Index

157